How to Succeed
in Middle Management

How to
Succeed in
Middle Management

George J. Lumsden

amacom

American Management Associations

Library of Congress Cataloging in Publication Data

Lumsden, George J.
  How to succeed in middle management.

  Includes index.
  1. Middle managers. 2. Management. 3. Organization.
I. Title.
HF5500.2.L849 1982   658.4'3   82-71323
ISBN 0-8144-5757-6

First Printing

To Jim, Nan, and Gary,
who still have this road to travel

Acknowledgments

Writing is often called the lonely profession. That is usually true—a typewriter has but one keyboard, and the person who sits at it has but one mind. Alone is often better. But there are times when an idea needs to be tested or a concept needs to be refined. It is then that one reaches for the telephone, pulls a knowledgeable and trusted colleague from important work, and draws on expertise and sensitivity not otherwise available.

I am indebted to a number of people who both agreed and disagreed with certain of my premises, but who ultimately helped me arrive at reasonable conclusions. Among them are many members of the National Society of Sales Training Executives—Bob Dies, Jim Evered, Morris Fockler, Don Frischmann, Ray Higgins, Bob Immel, Mel Kallett, Bill McGrath, Ian McLaughlin, Jack Slagle, and Bob Whyte.

A youthful view was provided by my son Jim, my daughter Nancy Sullivan, and her husband, Gary. They represent my MBA contingent. Credit goes, too, to my wife, Marge, whose many contacts with corporate wives shed light on the effects of middle management pressures and problems. The input from these sources was very helpful.

I cannot ignore the help and encouragement given me by former employees and employers and by a number of current clients who made it possible for me to study and experiment with many of the ideas expressed in the text. With their cooperation, theories became realities, at least in my own mind.

George J. Lumsden

Contents

I Complaints, Causes, and Concerns

1 Managing Managers: Building Bridges Between the
Factory Floor and the Executive Suite   3
2 Let's Compare Notes   11
3 If All Men Are Created Equal, Why Are Managers
So Special?   16

II Conflicts, Cases, and Corrections

4 Goals Are Nice, But Tasks Get the Job Done   29
5 My Boss Doesn't Ask *Me*, So Why Should I Ask *You?*   41
6 Of Course Someone's in Your Way—Me!   51
7 The Game Is Called "Simon Says . . ."   61
8 She Got the Biggest Piece, But You Got the Frosting   72
9 Why Is the Job Described One Way and the
Performance Measured Another?   84
10 I Know You Folks Are Busy, But This Is Really
Important   97
11 Shoulder to Shoulder . . . Until the Going Gets Tough   109
12 Of Course We Have a Training Department, But I
Don't Think It's in This Building   119
13 I Meant to Tell You, Lieutenant . . . Have the Troops
Explain the Battle Plan   131

III Styles, Studies, and Solutions

14 The More We Get Together, the Happier We'll Be   143
15 It May Look Good on Paper, But It Just Won't Work
   in My Business   158
16 Blue Sky and Solid Ground   166

IV Aptitudes, Attitudes, and Actions

17 The Best Conversations Require Two People and One
   Interesting Subject   179
18 The Best Meetings Involve Leadership, Participation,
   and Results   190
19 When You Prove You Can Stand on Your Own
   Two Feet, I'll Get Off Your Back!   200
20 Moving Targets Are Hard to Hit, But They Give You
   an Excuse When You Miss!   208
21 Participation Is a Two-Way Street   215
22 Management: Inexact Science, Unrefined Art   223

Part I
Complaints, Causes, and Concerns

1

Managing Managers: Building Bridges Between the Factory Floor and the Executive Suite

Ask any executive recruiter where the real substance of his or her business lies, and you'll be told that it's in finding good candidates to fill upper-middle to top management positions.

Ask any personnel director where his or her company loses truly valuable people, and the answer will generally be, "High-potential young managers who don't feel they're moving fast enough and upper-middle managers who have either bottomed out or want a change."

Ask the managers who move from one company to another why they left, and they'll tell you one of three things: They found the road ahead blocked by someone else. They saw a real potential for themselves at another company. *They thought their present company was neither taking full advantage of their talents nor rewarding them as they felt they should be,* no matter how they calculated the rewards—in compensation, opportunity, recognition, or challenge.

Tie all those findings together and you'll have a startling picture. What it tells us is that *many managers are not very well managed.* If they were, most companies would be able to shrink turnover, develop many of their top managers internally, and build management teams that work well—all the way from the factory floor to the executive suite.

Conversely, launch a discussion with some top managers in any number of companies about the turmoil in the ranks of middle management, and the responses may range all the way from, "Who says there's a problem?" to "The problem lies where it originates—with the middle managers themselves." Suggest to some top managers that middle managers don't feel they're being managed well, and you'll be told by a few that people in the middle are inept, they are resistant to change, and they have an altogether distorted perception of their importance.

I happen to believe that a strong case could be made for either point of view. And that's not a cop-out or an exercise in diplomacy. There are some in middle management roles who are not being used to full advantage and who are deprived of satisfactory opportunities. And there are others in middle management who aren't making a full contribution to the corporate effort, who enjoy the status quo, or who think they are worth much more than their performance indicates. To make matters worse, both kinds can be found in the same company and sometimes in the same department. That either condition is *allowed* to exist suggests a serious management fault, and that simply underscores my thesis: *Many managers are not well managed.*

For practical reasons, it would be wise at this point to define middle management. Some definitions include everyone above the first level of supervision (above line foreman, for example) up to the vice-presidential level. That's reasonably accurate, because it emphasizes the concept of a manager's managing *supervisory* personnel, not hourly workers. But that's looking at middle management from a large corporation's point of view. In smaller companies, a person may hold the title of vice-president and yet be operating at a middle management level in any number of ways.

Our concern here is the people who work below a policy-making level, but who have some say in how policy will be implemented and considerable involvement in carrying out that implementation. We are talking about those who manage the people who manage others. And through it all, we are reminded of the Rensis Likert linking-pin concept, which portrays managerial strata as arrangements in which people who are leaders in one group are followers in another. Middle management is a wide band, and it includes many people in a variety of work roles, line and staff alike.

Return now to the original theme that *many managers are not well managed.* At first blush this charge appears to be an indictment of *top* management. Not exclusively so. Poor managing is done in well-managed companies, and good managing is done in poorly managed companies. One quick observation is that wherever you find less than satisfactory middle management, you will find people who have difficulty defining their own roles or getting someone else to provide a definition. And when your own role is ill-defined, it follows that the role above and the role below are even more out of focus.

Actually, the individuals at either pole—top management or line workers—have no difficulty assessing their own roles. Owners or their appointed professional lead managers know that *they* run the show. And workers, for the most part, simply accept the fact that they're employed to perform a given task. Orders flow down, complaints flow up. But except in the smallest enterprises, company presidents don't tell production workers what to do or how to do it, and workers don't walk into presidents' offices with technical problems or personal grievances. Layers of management are stationed in between to implement the communications process and exercise various controls. Indeed, a lot may be happening in the middle of the string that will never come to the direct attention of either the president or the worker.

This is not to say that workers wouldn't prefer *getting* orders directly from the president, or that the president wouldn't prefer *giving* those orders directly. The most efficient businesses in existence today are precisely that—small companies run by a manager who knows what has to be done and staffed by workers who know how to do it. But for the most part, we left that kind of utopia behind us long ago.

So then, who created the intervening layers? The entrepreneur came to the conclusion that for him to (1) work less hard or (2) get more done, an assistant would have to handle some part of the workload. So what kind of person did he pick? You're absolutely right—someone who would:

Follow directions.
Be willing to do the kinds of things the president didn't like to do.
Be able to do things the president didn't do very well.

Now, of course, the president didn't tell the new assistant the whole story. The part about following directions, yes, but the rest, no. Which tells you right away how smart presidents are! And actually it was probably just as well, because the assistant, not realizing how valuable he was, followed directions. He even put up with a fair amount of browbeating by rationalizing that the boss wouldn't be critical if he didn't care so much.

All this went along beautifully until one day the *assistant* needed an assistant. In trying to match the worker specs with the job specs, the assistant wound up setting out the same criteria that had earlier been applied to him: Pick someone who will follow directions and on whom the less desirable or more baffling parts of the job can be dumped. Historians don't seem to chronicle these events very well, but probably the growth pattern was from shepherd to pasture foreman to flock superintendent to manager of sheep production to herd vice-president. Or maybe it was spice salesman to head merchant to chief of the tent to vice-president of the bazaar. Later on, it got really complicated!

This scheme would have continued to work well if we hadn't experienced a technological revolution. Now there were even more parts of the job that stymied the upper levels of management. Automation and computerization and all the rest of the technological advances made it next to impossible to reach down into the ranks for people to fill the jobs that required such specialized knowledge. Enter the college graduate. College graduates didn't *rise* to middle management; they *walked* right into it. They didn't progress from broom to lathe to lead operator to straw boss to foreman to manager. So they didn't know how lucky they were to be selected to fill a job that required them to:

Follow directions.
Be willing to do the kinds of things their boss didn't like to do.
Be able to do things their boss didn't do very well.

That's not all. Somewhere along the line in their educational programs, they were required to take courses in psychology. Although some of the fundamentals didn't stick very well, they *did* learn that there was a difference between motivation and manipulation. They also learned—and rightly so—that two could play at the same game, and that the manipulative manager, once spotted, could in turn be manipulated from below. Now the fat was *really* in the fire. The old dogs could bark, but what happened to their bite?

Meanwhile, other forces were at work. Among the many jobs top management chose *not* to do was to handle all the annoying details of personnel administration. What had started out as the employment office, with a file cabinet for attendance records, was now becoming a sophisticated operation. Not content to be mere interviewers and record keepers, the personnel people got to tinkering with the organization. Now we had organization charts and job descriptions and performance appraisals and attitude surveys and many other tools, called beneficial and appropriate by personnel administrators, time-consuming and irrelevant by plant managers and sales executives.

All this didn't happen just yesterday. We're talking about changes on the business scene that took place years ago and were well established during the post-World War II era. Given this, isn't it true that the old breed has long since vanished from the scene, to be replaced by the then-young invaders? You'd certainly think so, and you'd also expect that by now the modern management point of view would stretch clear from top to bottom in every corporate organization. But that isn't true, and those who can tell you the most about it are the people we're discussing in this book—the middle managers.

I don't believe we are talking about some sinister plot against a very significant and very vulnerable group of management people. Nor are we talking about a group of top managers who neither think nor care about what's afoot in their organizations. Many of them would be genuinely surprised to learn that all is not beer and skittles in the little offices a floor below. And others are undoubtedly working hard to make sure the unrest we'll be talking about doesn't break out under their roof.

What I do think we're dealing with is an inheritance of sorts. We tend to manage as we have been managed, and although we may be *conscious* of something we have been taught formally, we are likely to *behave* more in line with our experience. And since the executive suite is a prize to be sought, it is also a model to be copied. The fact that one doesn't do vice-presidential things down in a production office or out in a sales district doesn't seem to matter. The behavior is copied anyhow.

The linking-pin concept mentioned earlier applies here; that is, the idea that in a managerial hierarchy, the person who is a leader at one level is a subordinate at another. Hence, we tend to emulate the behavior above as we deal with our problems below. If the president tends to operate a certain way, the vice-presidents with whom he or she deals also tend to operate that way. But we must also bear in mind that those who rise to the top echelons of an organization become accustomed to operating from a power level unlike that available anywhere below them. Behavior can be copied, but power can't.

Yet what happens is that the behavior inheritance persists. As it is passed down deeper in the organization, sans power, such behavior begins not to work quite so well. And at lower levels it gets muddied even further because it's being used on individuals who don't understand it, aren't impressed by it, or are downright opposed to it. Also, as we go lower down the management string, we have to admit that the focal point of activity and concern is different than it is higher up. Above, it's the big picture, major goals and expectations. Below, it's a narrower view, more pinpointed goals, and a much more personal sense of what's happening.

As stated earlier, the people at the very top of an organization and the workers out in the field or on the line understand their own roles better than the manager who is somewhere in flight between the two. "I run this company" is simple to understand. "I drill bolt holes" is equally simple to understand. But, "I have a responsibility for getting a lot of people to do a lot of things, so that the product works and the company profits, and so on, and so on" is not quite so concretely defined. In many ways, the jobs in middle management are more complex, involve more activity and more relationships, and suffer more adverse consequences than any top *or* bottom jobs.

When Maslow defined his "hierarchy of needs"—a concept that showed that we move from one level of motivation to another: from physical to security needs, and from there to social, ego, and achievement needs—he noted that, as we move up on the scale, we are inclined to dismiss the importance of the need level from which we've just escaped. True, Maslow's was a different kind of study. But the same *can* be said of people who rise from worker to supervisor to manager to director to vice-president. Once in place at a higher level, it's easy to forget what it was like just one step below.

Just one step below. If that's where we focus our attention, then aren't we saying that *middle managers may not manage themselves—that is, other middle managers—all that well?* And doesn't that lead to the next logical question: *If we don't improve management in the middle, is there any hope of improving it at the top?* Because little guys sometimes get to be big shots, and they carry with them what they learned down below. So let's forget about trying to reform CEOs. The challenge lies in attempting to change behavior that takes place down at the levels where CEOs are born and bred. Never mind what takes place up in the boss's office; pay attention to what's happening in yours!

This book isn't intended to teach everything you'll need to know about how to manage. To be sure, we'll touch on skills whenever there's cause to do so. At the outset, the focus will be on helping middle managers understand themselves—where they are, what got them there, where they might be headed. We'll look at the nature of the middle manager's role and how it relates to other roles it touches. We'll discuss management styles, emphasizing the advantages of the more open, consultative, and participative style. Finally, we'll move into a few selected and related areas of skill that managers and managerial subordinates who want to rid themselves of the middle management criticism should develop. How-to and why-to will be blended together—if something's worth doing, the savvy manager will find a way to get it done.

Some of what follows will make you want to return to "Go" and learn the business all over again. Some of it will make you feel very good about what you're doing. If nothing else, it will make you think. And that alone may help you solve the middle management riddle!

2

Let's Compare Notes

My contention that many managers are not well managed is
derived from many sources. The first, most convenient, and most
readily understandable is personal experience. I have seen management close up. I have been part of it, above and below. I admit that
a considerable portion of my point of view is wholly subjective.
Another input came from conversations over the back fence or
waiting at the first tee. Managers live in neighborhoods where
other managers live, and they form social bonds with other managers from other companies. They gossip and complain and tell marvelous war stories.

And you can read about managerial woes in the papers. Sometimes it's boldly presented in an article or editorial, and sometimes
it's between the lines. If your local paper has a business section or a
column about people on the move, you'll read fragments that reflect the restlessness typical of modern managers. The classified ads
tell about it, too. People move from job to job for two reasons:
First, they think they'll like it better someplace else, because, second, they're not too satisfied where they are.

Books have been written on the subject. Magazine articles reveal
some research and some opinion. It's a subject for movies and television. Fiction tends to rise out of fact, reflecting the society in
which it exists, and many stories allude to Daddy's rough day at the
office. Dagwood Bumstead and Mr. Dithers have been at it for
years. Series like *Executive Suite, Network, Nine to Five, Dallas,*

Dynasty, and the daytime soaps are indicative of the way Hollywood likes to look in on the business world.

One of my concerns in writing this book was that my own experiences might not reflect the real world. I thought that my most recent observations of managers at work and in turmoil could very well be atypical; I left Chrysler Corporation in 1980 to launch a new career in writing and consulting. If ever there was a laboratory in which to study the problems of management, Chrysler provided it. But, I asked myself, were the problems there magnified beyond reality? So I surveyed a number of close friends—all professional management watchers and trainers—to check my conclusions and recommendations. They not only agreed that my track led in the right direction but also helped me lay a few more miles of it! I would openly credit each of them for their valuable input, but many requested anonymity. They're middle managers, you see.

I have worked in and around a number of corporations, some large, others small. General Electric Company gave me one kind of opportunity to see a slice of big-league middle management in action. A period of ad agency experience providing day-to-day contacts with clients like General Motors, Hoover, Brunswick, Cities Service, and others gave further exposure—superficial perhaps, but confirming. And then Chrysler. The good years in the 1960s, with major successes and solid profits, and then the 1970s, when it fell apart as fast as it had come together. In many ways, Chrysler was the best laboratory, because it had so much of the good . . . so much of the bad.

I mention these companies, not to hint that my goal is to kiss and tell, but to establish a climate of reality. In fact, names don't really matter, because the middle management muddle can be found on every hand. And it is not confined to major corporations; any company big enough to have two or three reporting levels is likely to have problems in the middle layers.

Nor is the problem one-sided. Some of what follows will stress middle management's frustration, annoyance, and dissatisfaction that is directed upward. But top management may have equal and opposite feelings about lower-level executives and managers. What is truly unfortunate is that the "solution" to this problem is quite frequently so wasteful. The dissatisfied manager quits, or the unsatisfactory manager is fired. To accept this is like saying that to make a marriage work we should have the divorce papers drawn up in advance.

My firm belief in the idea that many managers are not well managed comes from the fact that my work over the past 30 years has, in large part, been devoted to training people in the middle ranks. For 17 years at Chrysler, and subsequently in a number of consulting relationships, I had many opportunities to teach courses in communications skills, human relations, organizational effectiveness, motivation, decision making, and the like. It was almost predictable that somewhere in the process of explaining to supervisors and lower-level managers how to deal effectively with people under their supervision, the question would come up, "George, will *my boss* ever take this course?"

What these managers were telling me was, first, that they agreed with the substance of the course—that productivity was an end product of effective management—but, second, that the principles and practices so universally endorsed were not part of *their boss's* repertoire. How come? Is it appropriate to treat workers with dignity when no dignity is accorded the supervisor from above? Is it reasonable to require training for line operators and ignore the training needs of the supervisor? Communications theories are fine, but when the supervisor gets the latest dope from the shop steward, doesn't that show something isn't working?

Motivation is a prime example. We lecture the supervisor and the middle manager on bringing out the best in their subordinates by encouragement, instruction, and example. We teach them to motivate through counseling and to apply discipline with discretion. Then they parade into the boss's office and catch holy hell with no regard to ego protection and no opportunity for response.

We teach them to set and communicate goals and to build cooperation through understanding, but their bosses don't do either. We teach them to listen to suggestions from below and to let subordinates become part of the decision-making process, but their bosses never consult them in turn.

Want to talk about double standards? Want to talk about the problems in the middle layers? Some of the specific complaints lodged by men and women in the middle ranks are noted below. As you read them, bear in mind that we are talking about managers and supervisors—not at flag rank and not at the bottom level, but middle to upper-middle managers. People I've talked to and corresponded with seem to agree on the following as the key areas of frustration and discontent:

1. *Middle managers feel they're oversupervised.* They expect to be bossed, but not smothered. They'd like their direction to come in the form of goals to be reached, not tasks to be performed.

2. *They resent being saddled with responsibility without being accorded corresponding authority.* It's the old story of, "Do whatever it takes to get the job done, but *ask* me before you do anything."

3. *They believe they were placed in their present job without adequate training or opportunity to be trained.* This is particularly true in the first management role and/or in a switch to a wholly new type of departmental responsibility.

4. *They feel that they are not given the type of information and insights they need to perform properly, and sometimes lack vital direction.* In short, they may not want to be oversupervised, but neither do they appreciate undersupervision.

5. *They discover themselves being held accountable for action not covered in a job description, and being diverted from priority assignments to nonpriority activities.* With "extras" and "sidetracks," they find it difficult to do their own jobs the way they should be done.

6. *They dislike the fact that they're not involved in decision making.* Discontent on this score is particularly acute in areas where the subordinate manager has professional expertise.

7. *They feel that there are too many built-in restrictions and obstacles to personal advancement, growth, and opportunity.* Someone or something's always getting in their way.

8. *They smart over inequities in salaries and benefits, sometimes even over the lack of privilege they feel their rank deserves.* This perception is based on observations up, down, and across the management spectrum. And both inside and outside their companies.

9. *They believe top management often perceives the work they do and the department they run as necessary but not all that important.* And *they* think it is!

10. *When it comes down to the wire, they feel a lack of top management support.* This shows up in many ways—budgets, staff, interdepartmental cooperation, and recognition.

Review the above list quickly. It was compressed into a short form so that it could be examined as a bill of particulars, because that's precisely what it is. But note: These are not criticisms leveled at overall company policy. They are criticisms specifically aimed by middle managers *at management just one level above their own.*

Pause and ponder for a moment. If you feel this way about *your* present manager, how does the supervisor or subordinate manager *under you* feel about *you?* That's what was meant earlier by the statement that this book isn't intended for CEOs, but for any manager at any level! In future chapters, we'll be examining each of these complaints in more detail.

3

If All Men Are Created Equal, Why Are Managers So Special?

Opinions on the special nature of the manager or the unique concerns that are part of the management picture vary. There are those who say that the middle manager is really just a higher-level employee than some of the others—so it makes good sense to keep such a person just a trifle happier with a few extra dollars and a few extra benefits. Nothing exceptional, you know, but enough to calm the waters.

Others look at managers in the middle of the organizational hierarchy as people who already have an edge over the nonmanagers. Besides, aren't people in management the ones who are supposed to be on their way up? Isn't that an advantage? And who really cares if the manager in the middle does decide to pack up and go elsewhere? Don't we have a dozen people out in the shop or the sales force who would give an eye tooth to have a crack at the vacated job?

I've met more than a few top executives who see managers in the middle of the spectrum as losers to begin with. "How is it that I'm up here and she's down there?" "If Sam were such a ball of fire, he'd be up on this level by now, wouldn't he?" "I was a trainee in that same department when Charlie was a supervisor. Now he's just the manager, and I'm a vice-president. What's so special about Charlie?"

The question of why managers are so special has come up because it is the key to managing managers. The truth is that *managers have difficulty managing each other because they don't really understand each other.* Clashes of motives, goals, and expectations and differences in pressures and concerns all contribute to lack of understanding, both up and down. You've seen it happen, and so have I. Let's take an all-too-common case of intermanagement misunderstanding:

Jack is *state* sales manager. Above him is a *regional*-level manager. Next above is a director of *national* sales. Still above that is the *corporate* vice-president of sales and marketing. So Jack is four levels below the vice-president but also a few levels above the lowest job he has responsibility for. Jack is a bona fide manager, but he's a long way from the top. After all, doesn't he have supervisors, specialists, staff people, and sales representatives for whom he is responsible? Don't tell Jack he's not important to the management of the company!

Jack has been in his present job for five years. Before that, he was a salesman, field-training specialist, district manager, and assistant sales manager for the state. He has had several geographic moves in his career—from a sales job in an adjoining state to this office as a trainer, then out to a district for a few years, and then back to state headquarters. His concerns for his family are such that he feels further moves would be detrimental, and he is willing to forgo promotions in order to stay put. From a career point of view, that doesn't bother him. He likes what he is doing, does it well, and doesn't make much noise about his personal feelings.

His boss, the regional manager, isn't the least bit troubled by this. Of the five states included in his region, Jack's is the one that meets or exceeds quotas, gets reports in on time, and has been outstanding in the recruitment and development of new personnel. In conversations with Jack, the reluctance-to-move matter has come up, but only casually. Although Jack's boss has one state into which he'd like to move Jack to straighten out a bad situation, he has decided to leave well enough alone and take other measures in the troubled state. Reasonable understanding on the issue exists, at least at this level.

But the national sales director has another idea. He's not sure what keeps the regional manager from transferring Jack, but he thinks Jack has potential and *should* be moved around. Of course, the national sales director has, himself, gone through a number of chairs on his way to the top, and he feels that *moving around* is the only acceptable way to *move up* in business today. So he initiates action that really stirs up the pot: He *tells* the regional manager to move Jack into the headquarters in the troubled state. Here we go!

This entire scenario is played out in the most matter-of-fact way—nothing sinister and nothing threatening. It takes place when the national sales director and the regional manager are having dinner, and the subject of the troubled territory comes up. The conversation goes something like this:

"What are you doing to improve the situation over in Territory X?"

"I've gone over there a lot, and I think I'm beginning to see results."

"I'd move Jack over there if I were you. He'd handle it."

"True. But I'm not sure Jack would like to do that."

"Why not? It's a bigger state, has more potential. It's one grade higher than his present job, and he'd have bonus potential that would be worth plenty. Move him over."

"Yeah, but he's pretty well settled."

"Nonsense. Tell him. He'll jump at the chance. Everybody wants to get ahead."

The regional manager got where he is by paying attention and not making too many waves. He now feels threatened because the national sales director has his eye on the poor market, and the suggestion that Jack be moved into it comes across to him as an order. He has already demonstrated his own managerial weakness by not being able to handle the problem another way, so he saves his own hide by going directly to Jack with an order to move.

Jack doesn't want to go. He makes other suggestions. They go unheeded and eventually begin to smack of real insubordination. The situation gets reported to the national sales director, who phones Jack and puts pressure on him. Jack consents to take the other territory.

You have probably already written the balance of the scenario. Jack takes over the other office but doesn't move his family. He commutes for five weeks, but on the five weekends he explores job possibilities with friends in his own community. An attractive job offer comes up, and he takes it. The result: *Two* state headquarters suffer, the regional sales manager loses face, and the national sales director gets into hot water with the vice-president of sales.

Several worthwhile observations can be made regarding this breakdown in relationships. The key observation is that three managers whose jobs interrelate and who should rely on one another to their mutual advantage *don't understand each other.* That's the fundamental failure. The results of such misunderstanding, however, lead to losses and disruptions in the effective operation of the business that will require a lot of hard work to overcome. But what is most disturbing is that this type of error will be explained away in such a manner as to perpetuate rather than correct the underlying problem!

The national sales director—an eager, aggressive, and upwardly mobile executive—says, "I always thought Jack had the stuff that would make him a good regional manager. Now I'm sure I had him figured wrong. Just think—passing up a promotion just to satisfy a personal thing. Maybe we're just as well off without him."

The regional sales manager—a don't-stir-the-waters, hide-from-the-spotlight, boy-am-I-lucky-to-have-gotten-where-I-am manager—says, "I wish we hadn't lost Jack. But in the final analysis, he didn't help my situation any by quitting. I wouldn't have moved him if the boss hadn't said to. I follow orders; that's what got me where I am. Now what am I going to do about explaining this to people in Jack's organization? And what about the other state managers who used to look up to Jack?"

Jack says, "I never had a chance to explain my point of view. My objective with the company was to get to exactly where I was. I might have willingly accepted a move in two or three years, when the kids would be old enough to handle it, but not now. It wasn't a matter of putting myself before the company's needs, because I was doing a good job of handling the company's needs at this location. Just because others want to get ahead and make their way to head-quarters staff doesn't mean that those of us who stick to one job are wrong. Well, the truth is they never did appreciate what a good job I did for them all those years, anyhow."

Before we leave this case, a final observation: What was originally the *real* problem—the sales manager in the substandard terri-tory—is still there. And it is likely that nobody will want to tamper with that situation now because management is unwilling to have *two* open territories! So Joe Fumble will probably remain in place. *He may even rise in favor,* because he is loyal and will take orders—even if he doesn't really get the job done!

And how does that outcome affect the rest of the organization? For one thing, it suggests that keeping in line is more important than doing the job. In addition, the gossip among sales offices will have an undermining effect. Suggestion flow from the field to the regional or national office will slow to a trickle. People who have wondered whether to stay on with the company will begin to ex-plore alternatives. And even innocent managerial mistakes will be seen as calculated measures against the troops. The only good thing that results from Jack's leaving is that an opportunity opens up for someone below—a swap of the known for the unknown. Not much of a forward move for the company, is it?

In my opinion, middle managers are the lifeblood of any business organization. They anchor certain parts of an operation. They hold the business together at points where continuity is required. They make for stability and orderly growth. In most corporations, if middle managers are competent and reliable, you could broom the entire top floor, and the business would go on. They deserve to be helped, encouraged, directed, and rewarded, and they deserve to be understood. And that means on an *individual* basis. Not all managers in an enterprise aspire to the presidency, but that doesn't mean their present jobs aren't being well cared for. Some managers, by the very nature of their jobs, have little opportunity to travel, but that doesn't mean they wouldn't like to get out of the office on some worthwhile business assignments from time to time. Some managers carry out their jobs in relative obscurity, but that doesn't mean they wouldn't appreciate being featured sometime in the company house organ or invited to lead meetings where they could be seen and heard.

A fair number of upper-level managers don't seem to understand these things and show little regard for some of the jobs below them, even though they may have passed through those very jobs on their way to the top. Let me cite a few examples.

I worked closely with a corporation in which certain departments were almost totally managed by "pass-through" personnel. In other words, the managers on these staff-level assignments were field personnel who had been brought into corporate headquarters for a period of development and observation. A year or two on an assignment was par for the course. Then these managers were reassigned, back to a higher-level field position. There is nothing intrinsically wrong with this strategy, properly applied.

What *was* wrong in this case, however, was that a hard-working cadre of middle managers and specialists actually held the program together while these upwardly mobile managers passed through. Outside agencies and consultants provided the pass-through managers with ideas, and in-house subordinates carried out the tasks. Most management decisions were made on the basis of history, political expedience, and present convenience. The decisions worked because the resources to make them work were considerable—including both money and personnel, in the form of the cadre of experienced supervisors and specialists who were constantly in place. In many cases, I'm sure the manager of the moment never really understood what was taking place under him or her. Consequently, the manager looked back on the work of that department with little or no regard for the special skills and dedication that had made it operate successfully. The job was a piece of cake.

I once traveled with a Chrysler sales executive who confided in me that because his promotions had come so rapidly and he had had to spend so much time training himself on each of his current jobs, he scarcely had time to develop the people under him. And, he was honest enough to add, he never thought most of the jobs he held were all that important until after he had risen several levels above them. He was one of the few executives I've met who ever looked back, and I might note, he became a staunch advocate of training.

Conversely, another Chrysler executive persisted in the view that since he had made his way to the top by himself, why couldn't others? People in lower management jobs were, as he expressed it, "slobs." Training was something you did when there was nothing else to do, and he saw it as a vacation from the "real" work at hand. He never sought counsel from subordinates, because, "What would they know about it anyhow?" You can imagine what a splendid influence he was on middle managers within his reach!

Then there was the manager who felt that from the time he left his department and rose in the ranks, the work of that department had never again come up to his former standards. Consequently, he oversupervised his successors to the point that several transferred out, and others simply quit. The last time I checked, he was still looking for someone exactly like himself to fill the position. Frankly, the corporation hopes he doesn't find his ideal candidate: Two of a kind would be too much to contend with!

The object of criticism up to this point has not been the stupid or inept individual, but the truly talented one. We're not talking about losers, but winners! We're talking about successful people who have a blind spot that, left unattended, could ruin not only their careers but the careers of others. Lack of understanding is the simplest way to describe it.

For the moment, let's look at the argument that managers in the middle ranks are simply workers like everyone else. They already have built-in rewards and privileges, so why fuss over them any further? There are valid reasons for adopting an egalitarian point of view, but such a view doesn't jibe well with the business world. Managers have a unique characteristic built into their assignment—they are the only ones charged with multiplying effectiveness within an organization. Why, then, shouldn't they be paid some special attention?

I fully subscribe to the concepts of equal rights and equal treatment of individuals. But when we add to the equation the *un*equal factors of responsibility and contribution, we are forced to find ways to put things back in balance, so we increase pay and benefits as the levels of skill, care, effort, and accountability rise. It's done routinely in the skilled versus nonskilled levels, and we tend to assume it's also done quite routinely at supervisory, managerial, and executive levels. But is it?

The automotive industry pays its managers very well. Benefits of middle managers and executives are remarkably good. But, strangely enough, improvements in both sectors rely on the outcome of triennial negotiations with the United Auto Workers. At one extreme, top executives are so far removed from contractual agreements that, in their cases, the outcome doesn't make too much difference. At the other extreme, line supervisors, who have just moved out of the represented ranks, tend to encourage workers to "stick it to 'em, because what you get, I get." But middle-level managers—and they make up a very wide band—feel as though they are neither represented nor recognized. Despite better-than-average earnings, they complain because the system is too systematic. It does not recognize their special contribution.

Today's managers generally have received above-average educations. They have made significant investments in time and money to qualify themselves for entry-level management positions. They bring to the job, if not an already usable skill, a high level of developmental readiness. They move into the upward surge with great expectations for the future. They accept responsibility, partly because they know they are expected to do so, but also partly because they desire it. Goal-oriented and achievement-motivated, they present themselves for both service and opportunity. They give one to get the other.

Companies accept the fact that a newly appointed manager will take time to reach full productivity. They accept the fact that additional training may be necessary. Inherent in the overall concept of managerial progress through the ranks is the thought that somewhere in that group are the future vice-presidents and presidents of the company. This view is shared by top management and the managers in the upward stream. The selection/rejection process goes on. Some rise, some stand still, others leave.

To allow underdevelopment, particularly if the need for growth is there, is a waste of the organization's money. To allow potentially good managers to leave is a dead loss. Yet both seem to happen often in the middle ranks. Turnover takes its toll. Hiring, training, and orientation of new employees become corporate ways of life. But what is most unfortunate, in my own observation, is that somehow we let the really *good* ones get away.

Someone once said that every manager should be concerned about three jobs—the one he has, the one he hopes to get, and the one held by the individual who will replace him. (At the height of Chrysler's problems, we used to describe the three as the job you now have, the job of the guy you just laid off, and the job of the guy you'll lay off next week!) Most managers are pretty talented in building toward their own futures but not so good at building toward their replacements. Attention is focused up; focusing down is regarded as something that can wait. And it may well be that therein lie some of the problems in the middle ranks.

Management ranks require a lot of careful tending. Good managers don't just work by themselves—they multiply the effectiveness of others. Poor management relationships beget further poor relationships. Performance left unnoticed becomes performance that's not noticeable. Restlessness develops in the really good managers, and lethargy develops in those who aren't so good. What could have been a great management team instead becomes a collection of departing stars and resident benchwarmers. It happens.

Managing isn't so difficult if you do just a few of the right things. Managers often exaggerate the extent of their responsibility. I used to find myself claiming that I had 28 people in my department, just as I had heard others say that they had hundreds or thousands under their management. Not so. When I had 28 people in the department, I really had a management staff of 5. *They* were my prime responsibility, and in turn, each had 5 or 6 people to supervise. The day I discovered that I could manage the 5 and *they could manage the others,* I became a better manager. And they did, too!

Much has been said in the foregoing pages about attrition. I hasten to add a point based on personal conviction. I think *movement* in an organization is about as healthy a thing as can happen. To lose a valued manager isn't a problem, if that valued manager *stays somewhere in the company.* Once or twice in my managerial experience, other department managers approached me to ask if a particular individual was available for placement in their departments. I went after some of their personnel as well. Seeking opportunity for individuals within the organization is part of what a manager should do, and to have someone pirate your department is a compliment of a high order.

Movement within the organization makes for opportunity, and that's one thing uppermost in the mind of the manager who is worth something. It helps keep stagnation from setting in, provides a built-in motivational climate, and makes business life just a little more interesting. It's when you lose valuable managers to your competition that you know you've failed. Managers *are* special. When you can keep them that way, you're a very special manager yourself!

Part II
Conflicts, Cases,
and Corrections

4

Goals Are Nice, But Tasks Get the Job Done

The classical school of management has been around since the Industrial Revolution. It began with the discovery that workers assigned to specific tasks developed specialized skills and became so adept at performing those tasks that productivity increased. The assignment was the manager's prerogative, and to assign tasks *wisely* required planning. Planning meant setting objectives, dividing the overall job into workable tasks, organizing the available workforce to cover the various assignments, and defining the role of each person involved. That's how the organization chart and the job description came to be.

It must be remembered, however, that at the outset, managers and owners were one and the same. Products and services, by today's standards, were simple and uncomplicated. Workers, if not slaves, were nonetheless accustomed to taking orders. If someone said to do something, it was done, with no questions asked. Business organizations were small and easily controllable by a single manager.

As business grew, so did the supervisory problem. Assistant bosses came on stream, but they simply followed orders from on high as they gave orders to those down below. The system was a quasi-military one, in which people accepted orders in much the same way as did the famous Light Brigade: "Theirs not to make reply, theirs not to reason why. . . ." Undoubtedly, there were workers on the line—and supervisors, too—who saw a better way to do the job, but authority was vested in high places, and to challenge it was tantamount to treason. Of course, the passing centuries have completely worn away that old approach. Or have they?

Adam Smith was so taken with the idea of specialized assignments and division of labor that he described a situation in a pin factory employing ten men who, each assigned to a single task, managed to produce some 48,000 pins a day. Alone, according to Smith's estimates, they might not have been able to make 20 pins apiece. Smith's *Wealth of Nations*, published in 1776, is credited with being the first book on economics, but it was also the first to deal specifically with management planning. The minute you develop a new system that produces more than the old one did, you have set new goals and planned to meet them.

Frederick W. Taylor, around the turn of this century, launched the era of scientific management. He measured job operations, timed and evaluated them, made strict assignments of certain people to certain tasks, and in general, revolutionized the thinking of management. Here was planning at its very best, but it is important to remember that the planning was aimed at a labor level, not at a managerial level. And it must also be remembered that the management influence was applied at the line level, not above.

As industry became more sophisticated and more competitive, more goal setting and planning became necessary. And as the emphasis shifted from the small factory operation to the multiplant, multinational entities we know today, goal setting and planning came to require the support of highly trained specialists and data processing systems. Gone forever was the day when the name of the game was to work your hardest all day, then accept at the end of it whatever resulted. Or is it?

Before getting carried away on the magic carpet of modern management theory, I'd like to state a point of view: There is still a place in business for giving and taking orders—and following them. There are still right and wrong ways of doing certain things, and not doing them in the prescribed manner can lead to predictable problems. Managers who fail to insist that subordinates perform a job the *safe* way, the *quality* way, and the *quantity* way have fallen short of their mandate. To be permissive in a management role is to abdicate the role altogether.

Task assignment is relatively simple. You decide what has to be done, and you tell someone to do it. If it doesn't get done, you remove whoever didn't perform according to instructions and replace that person with someone else. If you're the boss of a gang of ditch diggers, you hand each one a shovel and tell them all to dig this deep, this wide, and in that direction. When the ditch is the right size and shape, you tell the gang to quit. Nothing to it.

But no self-respecting manager would take that kind of direction for ten minutes. Managers don't see themselves as errand runners, although they admit that sometimes errands have to be run. Because they're made of different stuff, they'll want to know why the errand is necessary. They're also likely to inquire about what else has to be done while they're out running the errand. Managers tend to think ahead of themselves, if they're the right kind of managers. *"Run and fetch"* doesn't pass the managerial litmus test. Managers always want to know more about the assignment for several reasons.

Good managers, through education or experience, have developed a sense of judgment. Let me admit, hastily, that not all managers make good judgments, but what we're saying is that managers feel they have a right to evaluate whatever they do on the basis of their own standards of what is proper, what is reasonable, and what is workable. One of my correspondents whose judgment I value highly claims that's one of the problems with managing managers—they think their title constitutes a blank check to operate beyond their charter. Modern management theory and practice, improperly communicated, may be responsible for that attitude. Nevertheless, the typical manager will not readily respond to task assignment without some hint of the reasons why.

Goals constitute much of the "reasons why." We perform this or that task because it is a necessary step toward attaining a certain goal. The goal makes the reasons for doing the task understandable. I may not like to go down into my basement, clean it, and paint the walls (tasks), but if it helps me sell the house (goal) and get a better price for it (goal), I attack the job with enthusiasm. I may not want to travel to an area sales office to work out problems with a field sales manager (task), but if I know that my presence there will salvage an account (goal) or help meet a sales quota (goal), I pack my bag immediately.

Goals put tasks into perspective. They're targets for achievement. Managers are, by definition, achievers. They need goals. Goals are the source of their enjoyment and the basis for their motivation. Middle managers, especially, need goals, because they are the conduit between upper-level policy and lower-level action. Goals matter throughout any organization.

If you went out to the golf course one Saturday morning and discovered that someone had taken down all the flags and tee markers, torn up all the scorecards, and suggested that you didn't have to play the holes in any particular order, you'd toss your clubs back in the car and go home. What fun is it when there isn't any par and you can't keep score? And what chaos there would be if people played the course in any random pattern they chose. We always like to know where we're going and when we've arrived there. Without order and without goals, it's no fun at all.

Every business I know of has some semblance of order and some type of goals. But I know a number of businesses whose employees aren't too sure what the objectives are, and where the plan seems to be built one day at a time. That's no fun at all, either!

This is a particularly sensitive issue at the middle management level. Here are managers—people of obvious talent who can be trusted with responsibility—and they cannot see purpose beyond the work piled up in front of them. They may not be in a position to set policy, but they will certainly be expected to implement it. They may not be in a position to design the product, but they will have to make it, sell it, or ship it. Their own little corner of the enterprise has room for imagination and creativity as well as for sheer labor. Goals exist, expressed or implied, at every level, and since managers are goal-oriented, they should be able to participate in setting them.

We forget that point sometimes in our busy moments, because it's simpler to call Bill in and tell him to handle this or that than to sit down and counsel him about goals. One of the middle managers' major complaints is that they're oversupervised. The minute I hear that complaint, I envision task-oriented upper-level managers who keep goals and plans to themselves and see their submanagers as assistants who merely divide the work the upper-level managers are ultimately responsible for. The result of such thinking is evident: As the manager, you parcel out jobs as they need to be done. Then you monitor each job to see whether or not it is coming along on schedule. But because you have assigned *tasks rather than goals,* you never let the subordinate managers feel that they are doing anything more than running errands.

I understand why upper-level managers do this, although I don't approve of the practice at all. Many managers are so intent on getting the job done, and done properly, that they use all the power at their disposal in the execution of their responsibility. What they forget is that they are dealing with people who feel that in their positions, *they* should wield some power, too. In some cases, this results in a collision of power; in others, there's a quiet resistance to it.

To put all this into perspective, let's look at the findings of dozens of behavioral scientists and their composite view of the kind of person who is attracted to, and succeeds at, managerial work.

Typical managers enjoy power and like to accomplish things and be rewarded accordingly. Money may be one reward, but position or prestige count even more. Money ultimately becomes a method of keeping score. Recognition for excellence in doing the job is a must, but it isn't everything. Typical managers want to work for both recognition *and* the rewards inherent in managerial activities.

Typical managers have a sense of responsibility to themselves, to their departments, and to the company. They see the success of the company as necessary to personal success and will extend their loyalties to that end. Recognizing that structure and order contribute to the success of an organization, typical managers want rules, policies, procedures, and lines of command. Aware that political influences can affect ease of accomplishment and ultimate success, most managers attempt to make as many friends and as few enemies among peers and superiors as possible. If they are not altogether unwise, the same effort will be made toward subordinates.

Managers typically cultivate skills that have a functional advantage—public speaking, decision making, planning and organizing, negotiating, and directing. To be personally successful, managers must be able to do those things that are clearly visible. And, finally, they actively seek an arena in which to demonstrate those skills to the kind of audience that really counts.

In general, the description just given fits all managers, from the lowest echelon to the executive suite. Obviously, the higher one goes in the organizational hierarchy, the easier it is to fulfill the native desires. But you'll agree that most of the things stated here fit you as you attempt to manage at whatever level you are privileged to do so. And the same is true for the managers you manage.

Most management textbooks correctly describe managerial jobs as involving a number of responsibilities: setting objectives, planning, policy making, organizing, staffing, directing, controlling, evaluating, decision making, and so forth. What is *not said well, if it is said at all,* is that the area in which these responsibilities can be exercised is *very limited;* that is, they apply only within the small circle of the manager's individual influence. And furthermore, even those objectives, decisions, and the like, that apply there are severely limited by overall corporate policy and procedure.

We often make a mistake in training lower- and middle-level managers when we teach them the skills but neglect to elaborate on the restrictions. And we compound the mistake when we don't establish a climate that allows them to make independent decisions *within* the parameters of their own sphere of influence. This means teaching all managers, at all levels, to share in planning and goal setting, and encouraging subordinate managers to do the same.

Rensis Likert's linking-pin concept applies again. The manager who heads one group is usually a subordinate in another, hence the *linking* pin. Managers lead sometimes and are led at other times. What I have observed over many years of managing and being managed is that if upper management includes its *next lower level* in goal setting and planning, the environment is set for passing that practice down the line. *But not always.* All it takes is one manager to break the chain, and you get involvement directed up, but not down. And that is a problem we have to address.

Let's make another quick observation. We're talking about two kinds of goals here. There are the major corporate goals that can be set only at the top. As an easy example, let's use *sales* objectives. The president of the company and his or her staff gather information on markets, competition, operating costs, and all the rest. The mathematics reveal a certain level of sales needed to support the operation, a higher level to make a profit, and still higher levels to make greater profits. That information, judiciously applied, will yield a corporate sales objective.

When that major objective is released, it spawns all kinds of minor objectives: product mix, geographic allocation, and that takes it right down to the individual sales representative. It's how these smaller goals are dealt with and communicated that makes the difference in whether or not the major goal is achieved. And that is the role of the whole spread of middle management.

This is the difference between strategic planning and tactical planning: strategy deals with the big picture, and tactics come face to face with the real world of getting the job done. One deals with what should be done, and the other deals with how to do it. These goals and plans meet somewhere if everything goes well. The concept was probably best expressed in the caption of an old cartoon: "When you're up to your duff in alligators, it's pretty hard to remember that your objective was to drain the swamp."

It might be helpful if once in a while the company president had to operate a plant or manage a regional office for a week. It might be equally good if a plant manager could hang around the president's office for a few days or if the regional sales manager could sit in with the vice-president of sales. Each would see how one kind of goal affected the other. The lower-level manager would see why the corporate goal made sense, and the upper-level manager would see some of the practical problems involved in fulfilling the goal.

There is a way, of course, of showing people how major and minor goals affect each other. By letting the circles of the various levels of management touch, the communications process would improve. If each manager would recognize that principle and involve subordinates in developing goals and plans as they relate to that particular department, some understanding would pass both ways. The only way middle managers will ever feel part of the entire corporate structure or upper managers will be able to rely on lower echelons to hold up their end of the responsibility is to have such a connection down and through the organization.

Chrysler Corporation suffered from this very oversight. It seldom connected its strategy with its tactics. It was either all strategy and no tactics, or all tactics and no strategy. Because tactics were always so evident, it often seemed as if they *were* the plan. Many managers who went through all the chairs in their progression to the top never learned the difference between long-range plans and short-range expediencies. Others never sat in lower-level chairs; they thought that setting an objective and making a plan automatically assured success. The lessons ultimately learned were very costly.

Interestingly, there were many well-managed organizations within that company. Although they frequently had to yield on issues of the moment, they were wise enough to recognize that over the long haul, they had to operate with both strategy and tactics of their own if they were to survive at all. What is reassuring about all this is that many of the managers who did such a superlative job of keeping their heads when others were rolling later moved to other companies, often taking on vice-presidential or presidential responsibilities. They had preserved themselves in middle management roles and developed other strong middle managers while doing it. They built a respect for middle management, because they understood what it was and what it accomplished!

Middle management is largely charged with implementing policies and seeing to it that direction is applied. That's the big reason for the concern about good management in the middle: It connects the two extremes and makes the wheels turn! And because it's middle managers who will ultimately move up to top management, the way they are managed is very important. They must be weaned away from the highly directive and classical management role of getting the work out and toward the wider view of overall goal achievement. If for no other reason than to develop the broader view, participative management must be encouraged in the middle echelons.

Of course, there are other reasons. Middle managers, if properly hired and suitably placed, have knowledge and experience that is valuable as *input* into any goal-setting or forward-planning procedure. Some of the old foxes in the department will point out the slippery rocks if only you'll ask them. Others will point out possibilities you never even dreamed of. It's sheer waste to use these people solely to *implement* plans you've developed all by yourself.

This chapter's title, "Goals Are Nice, but Tasks Get the Job Done," is absolutely true. But equally true is the fact that the tasks have little meaning unless the goals are understood. Add to that another thought: Managers who don't develop sensitivity and skill in discussing and establishing goals down in the middle of the organization can hardly be expected to be very good at it in the upper reaches of executive power. Still another reason for involving middle managers in goal setting: They, like you, want to be part of the big picture.

Take a hypothetical case: You're the manager of a department in which there are four subsections. Department title: advertising and public relations. Subsections: advertising, sales promotion, public relations, and sales support services. You report to the director of marketing.

You are asked, annually, to submit a forward plan of activities for the coming year. The plan is done concurrently with budget setting for the same period. You have been told not to expect a budget larger than last year's, and that, in turn, limits the year's activities. Since what you are currently doing appears to be working nicely, you could almost write next year's plan and budget by looking at the one from last year. Your four managers are very busy people. You come into direct contact with each of them on a daily basis. You know what they do, and they know what you want. You have a staff meeting every Monday morning, and you all go out together for a drink the last Friday of every month. A nice group and good relationships.

You came into the job a year and a half ago. Your predecessor, since retired, was a highly directive manager who seldom, if ever, consulted anyone. He wrote the forward plan and budget for the department without ever discussing it with you when you were manager of advertising. Your first stab at doing the plan was last year, and you were in a real time bind at the time, so you took one of the earlier submissions and penciled it around until it looked good enough to send upstairs. It was approved, and you went on about your business.

None of your four section managers showed any reaction when you told them a year ago what their budget limitations were. Obviously, you had managed to sell an adequate budget for the work planned. On the surface, at least, things are in good shape. In fact, as recently as last week, you asked each of the managers whether he or she needed any special budget consideration this year beyond an expected pad to cover inflationary costs, and each had said that the planned budget was satisfactory. Is there any reason to stir the pot?

The answer is yes. And there are two very different approaches to it. One is the Machiavellian approach of putting up a facade, maneuvering and manipulating so that people *think* they're being involved, holding back some information while parceling out other information, setting deadlines that don't allow much input, making a show of being more generous than should be expected, and in general, playing a charade. The other approach is recognizing that people know something, are capable of contributing, and will profit greatly by being involved.

You call a meeting. Someone remarks that is isn't Monday morning, and that tips you off to the fact that maybe you're a little too mechanical and routine in your management style. You tell your management staff that you are going to involve them in the planning and budgeting process for next year. "That's a great idea." "We've never done this before, but I like it." "I'll need to take a look at last year's plan before I even begin." "Mine will be a carbon copy of last year's; I already have a lot of things committed."

In this way, you involve your managers at two levels, individually and as a group. Before the meeting is over, you've given instructions on the kind of homework that will have to be done, the deadlines for turning in the material, and how the whole program will be discussed. You introduce an innovation: The general review session is scheduled to be held away from the office at a conference center, and you're going to pop for lunch and dinner. And you make one final suggestion: "Since we're going to try to be as comprehensive and far-reaching as we can in this effort, I'd suggest you involve some of your supervisors in developing your materials. Let's get this plan fine-tuned, so that when we send it in, we know we're on target."

You've done a variety of positive, worthwhile things: You've let your subordinates in on *your* responsibilities. You've opened the department's business to the whole staff. Nobody has to wonder what Sally's doing or how Sam's plan and budget will crack out. You've begun to weld individuals into a team. You've opened the door to an upward flow of communications. You've made a few managers *feel* like managers, and you've invited them to pass that down the line!

The foregoing case may seem like a neat piece of fiction. It's not. With adjustments in certain stage settings, it's a composite of experiences I've had myself, both as a subordinate and as a manager. It works wonderfully well. Here are some reasons why:

- Your managers, if they are truly responsible (and this is worth discovering), will submit *real* plans.
- Your managers, if they are at all prudent (and this, too, is worth discovering), will *prethink* the defense of those plans.
- They will probably suggest eliminating certain items of questionable value in an effort to justify adding activities they consider more worthwhile.
- They will reach further than you would have asked them to and commit themselves to projects you might have thought impossible.
- They will try harder to prove both the plan and themselves.
- They will compete with fellow managers, but they will also cooperate with them.
- They will see themselves as important parts of an overall plan and organization, but only as parts.
- They will see you and your problems, responsibilities, management style, and point of view in a new light.
- You will see them in pretty much that same new light, too.

Your managers—if they are worthy of the title—are achievement-oriented. They think in terms of goals and will work toward them. But they want to participate in setting those goals rather than just work toward goals you've already set for them. Control the process, but let them exercise creativity within that process. For all we know, Michelangelo might have become a plumber if all he had been allowed to do was paint by numbers!

5

My Boss Doesn't Ask Me, So Why Should I Ask You?

Many managers have a mind-set that makes them reluctant to seek advice. They will consult lawyers on legal problems and doctors on medical problems, but they will not consult their own staffs on matters that are just as specialized. To admit that you don't know or that yours is not the *only* point of view is often thought to pose a threat to the manager's position or status. Consultation is equated with weakness when, indeed, it is actually a strength.

This condition is perpetuated by the corporate system and structure. The middle manager who works under a highly directive upper-level manager feels it's impossible or impractical to manage in a style that's different from the way he or she is managed. Obviously, in a directive environment, orders passed down sometimes have to be followed to the letter, but even in the strictest hierarchy, there are many opportunities to manage differently down than up. "I don't dare ask you if my boss doesn't ask me" just doesn't make sense.

I recall many years ago being a very junior member of a staff. My whole concept of what big bosses did centered on the autocratic style, and I was very surprised when I was invited to a roundtable discussion with the general manager and his several department heads. In the first place, I felt very outranked, so you can imagine my astonishment when I was asked my opinion. Fortunately, I had one. I'm not sure how well I expressed it, but I still recall the manner in which that opinion was listened to, not only by the general manager, but by the others. Nobody interrupted, nobody commented pro or con, and nobody implied that what I was saying wasn't worth as much as what one of the senior members had said.

I can't remember the outcome of that session, but I can remember what it did for me. I felt stimulated. I felt a sense of worth. I would have gone to the very ends of the earth for the general manager, because he demonstrated real leadership. One day, after a number of such sessions, I asked one of the department managers whether such meetings were standard operating procedure throughout the company. He said, "There's no real policy on that, but it makes sense, doesn't it? I know the VP our boss reports to, and he's not much for consultation, but what difference does that make? Martin knows that he has to make the ultimate decision at this location, and he also knows that we have information that's valuable to him. Regardless of his boss's technique, Martin does what he knows works best for him . . . and for us."

In another staff experience, I found quite a different style. An up-from-the-ranks vice-president used to hold staff meetings—not to seek counsel, but to give orders. His meetings always began with, "We've decided to do this . . . this way. Now, Sam what do you have to say? Jack, what are your thoughts?" The meetings were short, because everyone around that table simply agreed. "Sounds good to me, Bill." And away we went.

If anyone offered a different point of view, it was quickly challenged. Seldom was a minority idea heard out to its full expression. Members of that staff fought little internal battles, vying for the boss's attention. If you ended up on the boss's side, you were in silk; if not, you were in burlap. Over a period of time, you learned not to speak up. Over a period of time, many crucial errors in plan and execution were evidenced.

Henry Ford, if we can believe some of the stories about him, was anything but a consultative manager. But he was smart enough to know that he didn't know everything. On one occasion, he was reported to have said that he didn't know how something worked, but that he could afford to hire someone who did. What brilliance! Somehow that should be planted in the minds of all managers: Don't expect to do it all by yourself; ask others for information and advice.

In the April 21, 1981, issue of the *Detroit Free Press,* a story appeared with the headline, "Burroughs Shakes Up Staff and Strategy." The article described W. Michael Blumenthal's move to decentralize Burroughs management and to "allow middle managers more voice in company policy." Blumenthal, you'll recall, was secretary of treasury in the Carter administration and a former CEO of Bendix. When he took over Burroughs, a Detroit-based computer and business-machine company, he took on a corporation that had experienced a 73 percent profit drop from 1979 to 1980. My guess is that he shopped around among his management personnel to find out why such a condition existed. After all, Mr. Blumenthal was new to the computer business. More than that, he was a seasoned and successful manager who knew the value of asking questions of subordinates. Apparently, he wasn't getting good answers.

The *Free Press* article went on to say that the reorganization was further intended to strengthen middle management, develop and retain talented executives, and so forth. The point is that unless the middle functions well and provides good information to the ultimate decision makers, corporate weaknesses are magnified. Strengthen the middle, and you strengthen the entire firm. Burroughs had historically been a top-dominated company, and the new CEO wanted to change that.

Lee Iacocca's takeover at Chrysler was a different story. Mr. Iacocca had been at the helm of Ford Motor Company until the man whose name was over the door decided to make a change. When Iacocca came to Chrysler, he knew the car business. Didn't have to ask anyone about it. Further, he lured away from Ford a number of his former colleagues and superimposed them on the old Chrysler management. He probably sought counsel from his inner circle, but there was little evidence of that trickling down to lower levels. It is unfortunate that upward information flow wasn't encouraged, because a number of costly errors could have been avoided—moves that made the corporation appear to be in even worse shape than it was.

George Odiorne, one of the best spokesmen on the subject of management by objectives, used to cite Lee Iacocca as a careful practitioner of the art of involving subordinates in planning and encouraging subordinate input. It's often the case that the formula that brought success is discarded in times of turmoil. At any rate, many Chrysler executives who understood that corporation's problems and had solutions that might have worked were never consulted. The master had failed to teach his first line of disciples the important skill. Or was it that they had the skill but failed to use it because it might threaten their image?

The net results were twofold: Many fine managers packed up and left, because it was too upsetting to continue in that environment. Others stayed on, some merely counting the days to retirement or a change in direction. Still others, to their credit, persisted in managing in an enlightened way, ignoring where possible the uncomfortable climate. But the losses of productive and creative managers were significant.

Managers at all levels seek involvement. This is often improperly interpreted as having a say in everything that goes on in the company. In truth, managers want involvement in matters that bear on *their* current role and in those matters that touch on *their* ultimate performance. Middle managers should be cautioned that *this is the extent to which they should expect involvement.* It's the manager's responsibility—indeed, his or her charter—to make that clear to subordinate managers. I may have an *opinion* about whether or not my company should carry on a given advertising campaign, but unless I'm in the advertising department, I can hardly expect to be consulted on it. On the other hand, if I *am* in the advertising department, it makes sense that someone would want to know my point of view.

However sensible that may seem, it doesn't always happen. One of my experiences as a training manager involved a sales manager who called me in to discuss the content of a training program we were about to launch. Now, it's the legitimate role of a sales manager to play a part in the training of the sales force, and I was delighted to have such interest shown. But instead of asking what our recommendations were, this manager opened the conference with, "Here's what I want done." Then he proceeded to outline a program that was not only ten years behind the times but showed complete disregard for the allotted time and budget. Even though we had conducted a training-needs analysis and had some outstanding program development people working on the project, he assumed the directive role without any concern for other points of view.

Annoyed as I was with his approach, I did what a lot of middle managers do and played the game. I took notes and listened intently. I asked a few questions that would lead him in my direction. Then I returned to my office and studied ways to make *my* program *look* like *his* program. A few superficial accommodating changes were made, but the original program remained almost intact. When it went back to him for review, he really thought he was reading his own program. When it was conducted, it was a success, and he was quick to point out to me that it was his idea. I figured if he was that dumb, I wouldn't waste time explaining it to him!

Recently, in a private consulting role, I found myself in a comparable situation, working with a sales manager who wanted training for his organization. That was as far as the similarity went. This time, the session was thoroughly open, with several subordinate managers fully involved in the discussion. The sales manager asked good questions and got square answers that addressed real needs. His key managers were relaxed and felt free to express themselves. We turned over a lot of rocks and found a lot of important things to do. The result was a program that was not only well designed but well supported by the organization.

Asking questions of your subordinates involves three elements: your willingness to be open to the input of others, your ability to ask the right kind of questions, and your ability to listen. Let's briefly examine all three:

The willingness to be open to input. First, you must be sure that expertise does exist within the organization. If it doesn't, then it's an entirely different problem—your selection or development of subordinates is below par. Look for strengths and use them; look for weaknesses and attempt to overcome them. But the minute you decide that your organization is capable of consultation, you should make up your mind to *use* people in that role. It doesn't mean you will be diluting your own power as manager. It doesn't mean—unless you go at it wrong—that you don't know anything about the problem or its solutions. It does mean that you are looking for the best possible solution your department is capable of producing. And when you have that attitude and express it clearly, you will have overcome all the negatives in sight. Out of that type of understanding will come a willingness on the part of everyone to proceed.

The ability to ask the right kind of questions. There are questions that seek information, questions that threaten, questions that trap, and questions that mislead. Ask only questions that seek information, and ask them in such a way that they can't be interpreted as any of the other types. The best way to avoid misunderstanding is to preface any question session with a statement of your overall purpose. Let people know, in advance, that you value their input. There are many ways you can do this without undermining your own status. Here are some examples:

• "As you know, about this time every year we get called on to put together a big sales promotion to clear out end-of-year inventories. We have a few good themes in the hopper, but since we have some advance-planning time available, maybe we'd like to try a different approach."

• "We've had an unusual amount of downtime in the plant in recent weeks, and it looks as though we have it pretty well stopped at the moment. However, it might be wise for us to look at some means of preventing it in the future . . . or handling it if it recurs."

- "Next week, we'll be involved in that huge annual mailing to our customers. I know that our plans are fairly well set, but it would be helpful if we talked it over in advance so that we know we have all the bases covered. And, it's possible that you may want to do a few things differently this year."

- "I'm in the process of preparing a report to go upstairs. In general, I know what I want to say, but you probably have some ideas that should be included. I can't promise to include everything in the report, but at least I'll know what you have in mind. That will be valuable in making the report complete."

None of the above suggests that the manager doesn't know which way to turn or that the input is merely a formality. All of them imply that attention will be paid to whatever is said. All of them invite cooperation and will bring people to your meeting with answers ready to fly. Now for the questions themselves:

- Ask questions that bring more of a response than yes or no. "What do you think about this design, Mary?" is better than "Do you like this design, Mary?"

- Ask questions that *don't lead* the response. "Charlie, what's *wrong* with this design?" suggests to Charlie that he'd better come up with a critical comment. Better to ask, "How do you feel about this design?"

- Ask questions that are constructive. In the case of the design, you discover that the response to it is generally negative. With that direction established, ask a question like, "Since you don't like this design, what do you feel would improve it?" That's better than "What's wrong with it?"

- Ask questions that show you want to get results, not test the individual. "I'd like to examine this design closely before I recommend it for final production. If you see anything that needs to be changed, can you give me those suggestions today?" That's better than "You're the guy who *should* know about all this, so if there are changes to be made, better give them to me before I recommend it to production."

Essentially, what you are after in consulting a subordinate manager is honest opinion and constructive advice. Ask the wrong kind of question, or ask it in a quizzing or threatening way, and you'll never get what you're looking for. I remember being invited to a *very* senior executive's office one day for a one-on-one meeting. He asked me for certain information, none of which I had on my person and some of which I didn't even have in my files. I told him that, but I offered to get what he wanted within the hour. I couldn't believe my ears when he said, "That's not necessary. I have a folder on that in my desk drawer."

My first inclination was to reach across the desk and grab him by the throat. Instead, I stood up and said, "Then let me send you *my* information, and you'll have something to compare with it." I left his office, pulled the data together, and sent my secretary up with it—within the hour. She came back with a short penciled note: "Thanks. J. R." I was incensed about the entire matter and asked another manager if he had ever had a similar experience with J. R. "Oh, sure. He'll put you on trial any time he has the chance. Be careful with that guy." Interestingly, my relationship with J. R. from that day on was very good; I kept a weather eye open for him, and he never again put me on trial. It's a moot question who was the winner!

The ability to listen. It makes little sense to ask questions unless you're willing and able to listen to the responses. Here are some very fundamental thoughts on the listening process:

• *Pay attention.* Let the other person *know* you're paying attention. That encourages him or her to give full expression.

• *Try not to interrupt.* Sometimes that's difficult, particularly if the other person is disorganized or lacks discipline. Stop the communication if it's off track, but let it run on if it's going in a reasonably good direction. Sometimes the best information comes after the unnecessary and irrelevant.

• *Probe.* If you feel that what you're getting isn't precisely what you want, ask interim questions that go deeper. "That's an interesting observation, Margaret. How did you come to that conclusion?" Asked in a nonthreatening way, that will yield additional insight.

• *Focus exclusively on the reception of information.* One of our listening faults is that too often we busy ourselves with constructing our own reply. Instead, try to listen to what is being said, with the sole purpose of understanding it. Rebuttal can come later. This skill, incidentally, is something you should teach your subordinates.

• *Learn to take simple word notes.* If you're sitting in your boss's office telling him something, and he has his head buried in a note pad during the conversation, you can guess that he's interested and taking note of what you're saying. But you can also be pretty sure that he's missing a lot of what's being said. Since a *single word* is often enough to remind you of a key idea, let single-word notes do in a conversational setting.

• *Make responses that let your subordinate know you've heard what was said.* A nod, a word of approval, an interim comment, then a summarizing statement at the end of the conference.

Many more things could be said about listening, but the foregoing will get you off to a good start. Indeed, if you do these few things well, you'll rake in prizes as the company's best listener!

As we leave this issue, let's take a look at what using subordinates in a consultative role does for you, the manager:

1. You'll find out things you didn't know before.
2. You'll discover how people feel about individual projects, their own work roles, the department, the company, and you.
3. You'll give your subordinates a sense of worth and a sense of contributing to the success of the business.
4. You'll learn from them what their capabilities are, who should be assigned to what responsibility, who can be developed beyond his or her present role, and who has the best judgment or the greatest insight.
5. You'll eliminate after-the-fact apologies and criticisms.

6. You'll *save* time by *spending* time in the right ways. It's easier to build a good mousetrap than to repair a bad one.
7. You'll build a team of productive subordinates who won't feel they're suffering from middle management neglect.

Obviously, you can't spend all your time in consultation with your managers, nor can they afford to spend all their time answering your questions. There's work out there to be done, and another meeting won't get it done any faster. But the constructive interpersonal relationships that are focused on doing the job better, faster, and more economically are worth developing. Furthermore, the basis for all *good* delegation lies in gaining good information and developing thorough understanding.

Even if your boss doesn't ask *you*, don't hesitate to ask *your* management team. You may get so good at managing that your boss will ask you the secret of your success!

6

Of Course Someone's in Your Way—Me!

Throughout the lore of behavioral science, there is one recurring theme on the subject of motivation: People will seek opportunity and will work to achieve it. People attracted to management are particularly opportunity-oriented. But what does that really mean? Does it mean that you, the manager, have to protect your own turf, build a moat around your castle, and discourage those who want to get ahead?

Some managers see it that way. Or if they don't, they give a mighty fine imitation of seeing it that way. They cut their subordinates off from other departments, are stingy with recognition and praise, are reluctant to invite an aide to an upper-level meeting, or are slow to change an organization chart by granting a new title or a higher pay grade. I knew a manager who never put names in the blocks on his organization chart, just titles; his argument was that it didn't matter *who* was in the organization, just *what* was being done!

Now there are two sides to the issue of organizational protocol and the who's-running-the-show problem. There *are* subordinates who make a manager's job difficult. There *are* subordinates who make moves that threaten authority. And there *are* people who would seek opportunity at the expense of their own manager, their manager's manager, and the entire corporation! I've had it happen to me, but it didn't go on for very long. That kind of nonsense must be stopped. But that doesn't mean that opportunity can't be sought through regular channels and in harmonious ways.

It's foolish to believe that personal growth can be achieved only by dislodging your superior or by waiting for him or her to quit, get fired, or get promoted. One of the attractions in large corporations is that lower-level managers can become higher-level managers without dislodging *anyone*. The price may include a lot of moving around, but if that seems worth it, the price is right! Yet even in large corporations, blind career choices may be made. Let's look at a typical case:

All the major domestic automobile manufacturers have field sales organizations that are similar: central staff, regional or area staffs, zone staffs. The terminology differs, but there are three levels of advancement possible. At the lowest level are the entry personnel—field sales representatives by whatever name they are called. Generally, new hires are considered trainees until they have been groomed sufficiently to take on a sales territory.

The first mistake that's made is telling the trainee that he or she will soon be a vice-president. That may sound like an exaggeration, but I've known it to happen. The next mistake is drawing a career line straight up through the sales organization. That may be the route to travel for some, but not for others. The third mistake, on the part of both the management and the young sales rep or trainee, is assuming that the beginner will be both capable of and interested in *management* work.

The name of the game gets to be "moving through the chairs." At times, the movement is so fast that the chair hardly gets properly warmed. Do well in a sales territory, and we'll send you to a larger and more sensitive territory. Do well there, and we'll bring you into the zone office for a tour of duty in one or two specialty areas—distribution, business management, promotion, for example. Don't get too interested in any of these staff functions, though, because your *opportunity* lies beyond that. The real truth is that it may be one's *undoing* rather than one's opportunity. But to find a niche in a specialty area, to do a bang-up job there, to want to keep on working in a specific role or in a specific location—these are literally the kiss of death.

The progression system itself isn't at fault, but the managers who monitor it often are. Many of the problems could be forestalled with some careful career planning and counseling, and others could be solved with less aggressive movement or movement based on more long-range thought. What about branching away from the specific sales organization into some of the specialty areas? For instance, a field sales promotion manager might well be taken into the central organization and developed further there. It happens sometimes, but not often enough, and the net result is usually restless, unhappy, and failure-bound middle managers.

The General Electric Company used to have a fine system of recruiting young men and women and placing them in corporate-wide training programs. The job rotation was grueling, but it worked well for both the trainee and the company. Year No. 1— four three-month assignments. See where you fit. Year No. 2—two six-month assignments. More exploration in depth. Year No. 3— two six-month assignments. Extensions of two areas of special interest. Then an off-program placement that met corporate and trainee needs. To be sure, that system reflected the luxury of the large corporation, but the same sort of approach might be used in considerably smaller outfits. And that type of rotation doesn't have to be restricted to the new or the young. Since when are organizations so set in concrete that temporary assignments and trades are out of the question?

Career planning as a corporate policy does seem to occur mostly in large companies. Recently, I counseled a young woman who was both schooled and experienced in the career planning field. She was unemployed. "When things are slow," she said, "management just doesn't want to invest in things that don't show up on the bottom line." I don't know of anything that will ultimately show up more on a bottom line than properly placed, highly motivated, predictably productive personnel. Do you?

Company policy or not, formal program or not, career planning and management counseling can and should be carried on by every manager. Beyond that, every manager should contribute to and actively encourage reasonable career opportunities for subordinates. It isn't easy, and it isn't always pleasant to lose a valued employee, but advancement should still be encouraged. The best managers I've ever worked under openly offered me to other organizations if the move meant opportunity for me and had value for the company. One did it so often that I asked him if he really wanted to get rid of me! His answer was close to the title of this chapter: "You're the logical candidate for this job, but I'm in it. The possibility that I'll stay in it is great. Merely because I'm here shouldn't mean that you can't get ahead. There are other things you can do and other departments in which you can make progress. If you want the opportunity, I'll seek it for you."

Fortunately for me, the job I was in kept growing, and I continued to be happy in it. On one or two occasions, I turned down offers and was happy I did. Just knowing that someone was in my corner helped. More than that, sensing such generosity above me, I felt free to offer similar opportunities to those under my own supervision. Sometimes the subordinates took the opportunity, and sometimes they refused it. But they *always* knew that opportunity was available, and they didn't have to wait for me to drop dead before it would come to them. That's the important feature of even the most informal career planning and counseling!

The openhandedness referred to here is one of the best assurances of continued loyalty. When a manager seeks opportunity for a subordinate, the relationship not only survives, but grows. That's true whether the individual goes to the new job or stays with the old one. But, consider the flip side of that situation, that is, a manager who denies opportunity or hides it from view. The resentment that builds can be a miniature version of hell itself. A former associate of mine was once kept from learning about an opportunity within his own company. He didn't find out until the position had been filled by someone else, and he was told by the manager who had had the opening, "I asked Jerry if I could bring you in for an interview, but he told me you weren't interested." The subsequent argument wasn't for tender ears, and the ending wasn't particularly pleasant. A good manager's career upset by a poor manager's self-ishness.

Let's take a closer look at career planning and counseling in terms of practical management application. Here are some simple steps all managers can and should take with respect to their subordinates:

• *Don't plan someone else's career.* Among the most unhappy people I've known are men and women who listened too hard and too long to a parent or a teacher. That's not to say parents and teachers—and managers—have no role to play in the development of people within their sphere of influence, but it does mean that I can't make up your mind and that I can't live your life. Unfortunately, taking over seems to go with the territory in the minds of many managers. "If I were you . . ." is a ridiculous beginning to any statement, because *I'm not!*

To counsel doesn't mean to dictate. Far from it. To counsel means to explore, to provide information, to aid in the thought process of others. In many cases, it means nothing more than lending a sympathetic ear. In all cases, it means approaching others with questions directed at *their* interests and needs, not our own preju-dices. Help, but don't direct.

• *Show people the possibilities.* Plot out all the avenues available to your subordinates, indicating the ones within your operation as well as those you know about elsewhere. Be frank about what seem to be closed doors, but don't nail those doors shut. Your position and your experience should have shown you a lot of things about your company that you can pass on to a subordinate. The more in-formation, the better the ultimate plan.

Offering career advice is really nothing more than itemizing available options as to desirable and undesirable ones, with each option having its own price tag. Wise shoppers, particularly young ones with options still open, sample before they buy. As wise sell-ers, managers should expect this and shouldn't pressure subordi-nates to commit themselves early to a career path.

The important thing in career counseling is to do it. By showing interest in your subordinates, you're doing them a great favor. When they indicate a direction they'd like to pursue, be honest about your appraisal of it and offer help if you can provide it.

• *Get subordinates to take a hard look at themselves.* In many ways, becoming involved in career-path design for a subordinate offers you a good shot at subtle performance correction. But to use a career-counseling session as an excuse to chew someone out is self-defeating, so never confuse the two.

When you ask managers where they expect to be, say, three years from now, don't be surprised to get responses from both ends of the spectrum. "I guess I'll be right here, doing what I'm doing," may be one extreme. "I expect that in three years you'll be promoted, and I'd like to be sitting in your chair," may be the other. That answer is your signal to begin asking questions that make the other person look at qualifications and at real career objectives. "Is that what you'd *like* to do?" "Will you be *ready* to make that kind of move?" "Do you realize that some *personal inconvenience* may be ahead with a plan like that?" "What happens if you *don't* realize that ambition in that sort of time frame?" "What *alternatives* do you have in mind that might be acceptable to you?"

Many companies, even if it goes unpublicized, have de facto qualification barriers to certain kinds of promotions. Lack of a college degree may be one such barrier. For some higher posts, lack of an advanced degree may be another. Lack of certain work experience—going through the chairs—may be still another. Try as you may, it could be difficult to break down some of these qualification prejudices. While it's not the manager's role to pronounce judgment, it *is* appropriate to provide warnings.

In no way should career planning become a major spoon-feeding of subordinates. But many managers, particularly the younger men and women in your organization, have no one else to talk to about these matters. And who besides you could respond with more practical information and advice?

• *Promise nothing.* Who knows what tomorrow will do to your own situation? Who knows whether some major change in the corporate structure may negate whatever arrangements you have in mind? Who knows what the subordinate may do in terms of performance or personal plans to turn the tables completely? It's right to expect the subordinate to move into a career path and for you to help make that objective attainable, but it's dead wrong to make promises.

One of my long-time acquaintances described a situation in which as assistant manager was very much in favor with his boss, who intended to retire within two or three months. The boss called the assistant in and told him that he had been recommended for the promotion. "I'm sure you'll get it, Jim," said the manager. "Just plan on it." At the time, the maintenance crew was moving through the building redecorating offices. Since company policy allowed managers to select their own paint colors from an approved list, the assistant was allowed to pick *his* color, because the office was certainly going to be his in a matter of weeks. You guessed it: A young lion from central staff was sent down to take over the department—a rotational assignment for "seasoning," I think they called it.

Whoever said that nothing is certain but death and taxes was absolutely correct! Ditto Murphy's Law.

• *Arrange time for periodic review.* If all is going well, maybe the performance-review session is the right time to look over the entire situation. If it isn't, then why not do it another time? One session on career pathing isn't enough anyhow. Keep notes on the original career-planning session and update them from time to time. Your circumstances may change, the original plan may change, or you may change your mind about supporting that plan.

• *Communicate some elements of the plan to others who may be in a position to make it materialize.* Something like the following scenario might be possible:

You're having lunch with the director of the marketing-data department. Vicki Anderson, one of your supervisors, has a fine background in sales but at one time also did advertising research for a major advertising agency. She has made an excellent contribution to your organization, but because of family considerations, she doesn't want to be transferred, so you feel that promoting her within your own sales organization has some built-in limitations. She knows that and isn't making any fuss over it. But she *deserves* an opportunity. You mention that to the director, who replies: "There's nothing open in my area at the moment, Charlie, but in the next several months, we may be making some moves. If your young woman has had some statistical experience, maybe she'd work out nicely in a slot I may have to fill. It's a grade or two higher than the one she has, and we'd welcome somebody who can bring some real field experience to the job. Don't raise any false hopes for her, but the next time I'm in your office, point her out to me and send up a copy of her personal history record. Meanwhile, sound her out on the general idea. When I know better where we're going, I'll interview her."

I've been in on luncheon conversations like that which have turned careers, departments, and even divisions in new directions. It all starts with open discussion.

Professional career counselors could probably add many other pieces of good advice to the above list, but you'll find these practical and easy to implement. And if you have no formal program or no professional personnel staff to give you further guidance, they may prove especially helpful in getting you off to a sensible start.

A word of caution: Not every subordinate burns with ambition to go on to bigger and better things. The willingness to stay in the same position does not always imply *lack* of ambition. Here we have, however, a very valid reason for career counseling: It often distinguishes between the person who has already reached a career goal and is getting satisfaction out of becoming more and more expert in a narrow field and the person who doesn't know what he or she wants or doesn't dare to go beyond the present job. Counseling will differentiate between the two and may often uncover interesting points of view that make managing someone more effective and more comfortable. What *would* you do if all the members of your department were eyeing the presidency, or even your own job?

The benefits your subordinate managers derive from career planning are obvious, even when it's done on as elementary a basis as described here. But that's not all. There are advantages in it for you, too. Here are a few benefits on both sides of the equation:

Benefits for your subordinate managers and supervisors include:

o A feeling that you, their manager, are really concerned and are in their corner, that you're as much a friend as a boss and are willing to help if they want or merit it.

o A larger view of opportunities afforded in your department or your company, beyond the immediate limitations of the present situation.

o An understanding of what it will take, what your subordinates will have to do, and what you'll be looking for in their performance if they aspire to better things.

o A recognition that roadblocks and dead-ends may spring up that are beyond their control . . . or yours.

Benefits for you, the manager, include:

o Splendid insights into aspirations and goals of subordinates, which may provide excellent clues to how to motivate them.

o A track to follow in making assignments and granting both responsibility and authority.

o An opportunity for contact that may minimize the need for future corrective and disciplinary actions.

o An end to I-win/you-lose management on both sides. I-win/you-win is not only more productive but more comfortable to live with.

Climbing the management pyramid is an interesting life-exercise. It gets narrower toward the top, presenting fewer opportunities but also fewer surprises. That's probably why managers in the very upper layers don't expect much career-planning assistance from their bosses. That's probably why your boss doesn't counsel you: He or she feels you're already on your way and know where you want to go. It's a reasonable conclusion.

No matter. Even if you were never counseled on this subject, don't let that dissuade you from introducing it below. That's where it's needed and where it will help the most. It's an easy way to silence one of the most frequent laments of the middle manager— "Nobody cares." Care, and your department will be all the better for it!

7

The Game Is Called
"Simon Says . . ."

Traditionally, management has been defined as "getting things done through others." Without question, we recognize that a manager has not only the right but the responsibility to direct others toward the doing of tasks. We unhesitatingly accept the fact that the manager is also expected to control, discipline, and reward according to the performance delivered. Yet middle managers continually complain that they are oversupervised or undersupervised. Why?

If you have ever been oversupervised, you can list a bill of particulars:

- You were awarded the task, but you also got instructions, chapter and verse, covering every aspect of it.
- Even with all the instructions, your manager still hovered around and even took over at times. ("Please, Mother, I'd rather do it myself.")
- Your mistakes were reprimanded, but your successes were overlooked.
- Even on subsequent assignments to perform the identical task, your manager's domination interfered, so that you never felt wholly on your own.

If you have ever been undersupervised, you can also make a complaint list:

- You knew, in general, what had to be done, but no importance was ever attached to the assignment.
- You did the required work—sometimes even very well—but no mention was ever made of the achievement.
- If the project didn't come off well, you were criticized but never in a constructive way—this is what went wrong, and *why.*
- Reports you made on completion of a project received little or no mention, so you made subsequent reports shorter—then quit making them.

The end result of both oversupervision and undersupervision is that employees begin to get the sense of inadequacy or unimportance. There is the feeling that the manager doesn't trust them with an assignment or trusts them only with insignificant ones. Self-worth is in the balance, and when that happens, watch out!

At the heart of this problem is the manager's ability—and willingness—to delegate. Since we are discussing the job of managing managers, let's consider the issue from both levels, up as well as down. Middle managers delegate and are delegated to, so cautions are needed in both directions.

Some managers fail to delegate or delegate poorly for a number of reasons:

- They feel threatened: What if the subordinate does this so well that he or she is noticed?
- They honestly don't believe that anyone in the organization can do the job as well as *they* can.
- They simply enjoy doing certain things and wouldn't think of letting someone else in on the fun.
- They have a fuzzy conception of the managerial role and aren't much concerned about it. After all, when they were foremen they always did it this way.

We can snicker at some of these responses, but they are understandable reactions on the part of some managers. There *are* people in the middle of organizations who will not exceed their authority but will capitalize on the glory. There *are* organizations—blame it on an inheritance from a previous manager—in which incompetence prevents some delegation. It *is* fun to do some things by yourself, and who says that managers can't get in on the act from time to time? Only the final reason—never growing out of an earlier experience—can be held up to ridicule. And that, in a nutshell, is what lies behind most of the improper managing of managers—misconception and habit.

In dealing with their superiors and subordinates alike, managers at all levels should:

- Minimize threats by directing behavior toward job performance and letting the credit come naturally.
- Prepare to handle responsibility and try to be the one to whom the job is delegated. There's a little selling connected with this.
- Learn to let go, but continue to stay aware.

If I'm your subordinate, I may not want you looking over my shoulder as I work on the task you've assigned me, but neither do I want you to separate yourself to such an extent that you don't know what I'm doing. And this brings up another topic. Managers should recognize that delegation comes in a number of shapes and sizes. In fact, there's little wrong with giving responsibility *without* authority, if the guidelines are drawn properly. Here's a simple example of what I call *limited* delegation:

I am a member of your staff. A problem arises that comes to your attention. Neither you nor I know precisely what the problem is or what its ramifications might be. Let's say we have a dissatisfied customer who has written in with numerous complaints in a typical, if not classic, emotional letter. Because the letter bypassed the normal district-to-region-to-home-office circuit, you want to explore it further rather than buck it back down to the appropriate level. You say to me, "George, check on this and give me some additional information. Then we'll decide what to do."

I have been given a responsibility *but no authority to act.* So I exercise some judgment, call the office that should normally take care of such matters, ask them if they're aware that the complaint exists, get all the information, and report back to you. I report that the office had dealt with this particular customer before and thought the matter had been handled but will get back on the case immediately. If that suits you, the project is ended. If not, you may give me further directions or *provisional* delegation.

You say, "Call the office back and tell them to hold off on this for a few hours. I think there may be some serious implications in a complaint of this nature, and it had better be handled extremely well. Talk it over with the manager out in the field and come up with some recommendations on how the thing should be taken care of. Then we'll decide what to do."

I now have an enlarged responsibility, but my only authority is to discuss it with appropriate people. I still have no mandate to act *fully* on the problem. Unless the situation is so obviously ridiculous that it could have been handled by a single phone call to the customer, I defer to your judgment without any rancor. I discuss it with the field manager, we come to an agreement and develop a proposed plan of action, and I report the same to you.

Now you say, "Fine. Call Bill and have him handle it as you suggested. And tell him if a situation like this arises in the future, to take care of it in the same way. I'd also like a report on this and on any other similar cases when they've been put to rest." That is what is called *full* delegation.

In delegating, managers sometimes have to go through the series—*limited* first, then *provisional*—before finally according *full* delegation on a regular basis.

The fact that you want to be informed *after* action has been taken does not demonstrate lack of trust but rather *real* trust coupled with *interest*. The key to all this is the manner in which it's communicated and the prior understanding of the limitations. These three levels of delegation would be a fine subject for discussion with a managerial staff or a good topic for a memorandum. The game goes better if the rules are established beforehand.

An earlier point, that of allowing others to share in planning, is relevant here. The ease of delegating relates directly to the practice of involving subordinates in setting goals. Managers who see in other managers a capacity for independent action are more likely to delegate freely than nonparticipative managers. Also, managers who are involved in planning and decision making by their own managers gain greater understanding of goals and acceptable procedures. The combination of the two—the subordinates' capacity for independent action and the manager's understanding of the process of delegation—create a very comfortable climate for full delegation. It is important that this be felt on both sides, by the superior and the subordinate alike.

Part of delegation, after all, is communicating a clear set of performance objectives. But it should never be left at that. If someone were to press me for the simplest description of a manager's responsibilities, I would boil it down to two terms: "direction" and "support." Delegation should include those two concerns—good signals plus the presence of help wherever and whenever needed. Managers who feel they are *over*supervised are the recipients of a lot of direction, but the "support" is really just more direction, not true support. Managers who feel they are *under*supervised generally receive poor direction and no support at all. Little wonder they register dissatisfaction.

We must bear in mind that the whole issue of delegation involves some subtle considerations. Some managers will not delegate because they question their subordinates' abilities and judgment. This situation is a clear signal for training and counseling. If you dare not cut me loose on a project because you think I might botch it, you owe me an opportunity to learn, and if need be, to teach me yourself. I would take such instruction gladly if you approached me with, "Since I'd like to give you the responsibility and authority to take over these projects, we'll spend some time together going over the steps, so that *you're* sure to *succeed* and *I'm* sure to be satisfied with the *results.*" I couldn't be offended by that, nor could I be offended if the break from total supervision came in reasonably measured steps. I *would* be offended if I were never taught and never given the chance to show what I could do.

As a manager, I have been guilty of not delegating for all the reasons given earlier. When a certain activity would take place *just once*, for instance, it was simpler to handle it myself than to teach someone else to do it. I defend that as a good business judgment. But over many years, I learned that the more I delegated, the more competent and responsible people were capable of being. Furthermore, with few exceptions, subordinate managers liked it. On those few occasions when someone faulted and I took the blame, I chalked it up to a good learning experience for all concerned. One incident involved a subordinate who assumed more authority than he should have. We wound up starting back at square one—*limited*, then *provisional*, and finally *full* delegation once the air had been cleared.

Not long ago, I had a curbstone conversation with a friend who is a retired advertising agency executive. He told me a story that is worth retelling, because it illustrates the consequences of delegation. The story focuses on who's the boss and who takes the blame—all-important considerations in the manager's feelings about delegating and being delegated to.

My friend managed a branch office of a major national ad agency in a city about 200 miles away from the home office. He had a staff of nearly 50 people and some very important accounts to handle. An ad for one of those accounts hit the media nationally and, of course, showed up in the home office's local paper. As luck would have it, the ad contained an error, and the phones began to ring. "What about this?" "What's going to be done to correct it?" "Who did it?" and so forth. As he described it, my friend, a quiet man now many years removed from the incident, still showed the emotional intensity of that occasion.

He explained to his superior that he was aware of the error, that it had been corrected and the client was satisfied, and that business was back to normal. He also added that, before the incident, precautions had been taken to prevent such an error, and that now, still more precautions were being taken to see that it didn't happen again. Then came the big question: "Who was responsible, and are you going to can the so-and-so?" This was the perfect opportunity for laying off blame. My friend didn't.

He told his boss that *he* was responsible. The boss said that was impossible, since he managed the branch and didn't actually write the ad. True, my friend replied, but that didn't make any difference. *All* work was delegated to someone in one way or another, and the person who had the close-up responsibility was a thoroughly capable individual but had made an error. It had been discussed with everyone, everyone regretted it, people had worked overtime on their own to rectify the situation, and the office was back to normal . . . as was the client.

The boss asked again for the name of the person involved and hinted strongly that there should be a firing. My friend resisted quietly by saying, "When you sent me here to handle this office, you gave me a responsibility and the authority to back it up. Fire me, and then you can work your way down to the person who made the mistake. Otherwise, please let the matter rest where it is."

"So you got fired," I said.

"No," replied my friend. "That was the end of it. If it had been pushed any further, I would have quit, but that never happened."

"Was your boss vindictive in any way?"

"No," he said. "We got along very nicely for a long time afterward. He just had to be reminded that business, properly run, involves spreading responsibility. He realized that he would have cut off creativity and incentive if he had pressed the matter further. He was a very wise manager."

My friend was fortunate. What might have happened was the classic hopscotch routine, in which Mr. Home Office flies out, conducts his own investigation, gets in on the act, bypasses the manager's authority, and undermines it forever. That happens all too often.

Another friend, who is still in the middle management milieu, also has an illustration of delegation, but it's a rather different kind of story. His own manager had always insisted that my friend personally attend to setting up certain meetings. A great deal of importance was attached to these events, and everything had to be perfect. Because under ordinary circumstances, the task wasn't very difficult, my friend, a department manager, simply did it himself. He shouldn't have. It was a job that wasted time that he should have been spending on planning, organizing, directing, and supervising others. Habit and deference to the dictates of the boss had nonetheless kept him doing it.

One day, just as the planning and preparation for another big meeting was about to begin, my friend found that he would have to be on the road when he would normally be handling the minutiae of the meeting setup. Doing the job personally was now next to impossible, so he called in Sally Jackson, one of his supervisors, indicated to her the importance of the job, explained the preparation procedures, and left town. Whenever he called in, his subordinate cheerfully reported what good progress was being made. Everything sounded completely on track.

It couldn't be going that smoothly. It never had. There were always some last-minute changes required. What if Sally had overlooked something? But what do you do when you're on the other side of the continent? Worry seemed appropriate, so my friend did a whole lot of it. As it turned out, his worry was wasted, because Sally had taken on the job, exercised her proper authority, and fulfilled her responsibility perfectly. The meeting turned out to be a huge success.

"I learned two things," the department manager said later. "First, the job that had been delegated to me could have—and should have—been delegated downward, and my role should have been supervisory. I simply took the assignment as my own, and that was a mistake. In fact, I think my boss probably wondered why I did it, even though he had made quite a point of its importance. Although everything went perfectly, I believe that even if there had been a slip-up or two, I wouldn't have been challenged about giving the assignment to Sally.

"The second thing I learned was that Sally had capabilities beyond those I'd previously noticed. She got scripts written and slides made every bit as well as I would have. Of course, earlier she had done less important assignments in that area, but nothing quite so much in the spotlight. This occasion allowed her to put her ideas to work, and she was concerned enough to make sure everything went well. From here on, I'll broaden her responsibilities with considerable confidence. Too bad it took an emergency to make it happen."

Let's look at some of the key steps that make delegation work:

o Have goals for the total activity of the entire department. This means long-range planning far in advance of the action.
o Involve your immediate subordinates in the planning, so that they see the big picture.
o Make sure that everyone is fully assigned to major chunks of the work. Balance the load.
o Make sure that each individual is fully capable of performing his or her specific role.
o Analyze the capabilities of each individual with the thought of expanding the role or, in case of an emergency, co-opting services for someone else's support. This may mean training and counseling.
o Let it be known that, unless otherwise assigned, your subordinates have standing assignments, with full responsibility and corresponding authority.
o Let it also be known that, from time to time, special assignments will be made, sometimes considerably beyond the subordinates' job descriptions.
o Arrange for individual conferences for both specific assignments and personal development.
o Follow the activity.
o In regular staff sessions, acknowledge good work and individualize your comments.
o In the event of problems, work separately with people, pro-

viding support as required and making criticism as private as possible.

○ Periodically, require that all subordinate managers report progress not only to you but to the staff.

○ In all of this, be willing to accept the fact that not everyone attacks a problem the way you might; results are more important than method, unless the method being used is *obviously* wrong and destined to fail. In the end, you are accountable for everything that goes on in your department, and you have the right to insist on acceptable procedures. But watch before you make the judgment.

An interesting thing about delegation is that it puts the manager more in charge when it's done on a broad basis than when it's done on a parcel-out basis. The broad approach gives the manager more time to plan, to supervise, and to maintain control.

Effective delegation to managers under your control does the following things for you:

○ It lets you balance the workload, including your own.

○ It gives you insight into individual strengths and weaknesses.

○ It frees you to do things that make your operation move ahead rather than just keep pace.

○ It gives you time to do better planning.

○ It lets you interact with other department heads so that you get a more comprehensive picture of the overall operation.

○ It makes you a more effective subordinate to your own boss and gets your influence flowing upward as well as laterally and downward.

What effective delegation will do for those under your supervision is equally important:

○ They'll gain a level of self-respect that will increase their concern for exercising skill, care, and effort on the job.

○ They'll perform to the extent that you accord them more freedom and encourage more creativity.

o They'll learn to make good decisions, because they know that you're monitoring results and that results are traceable to decisions.

o They'll compete with others for your approval, but not at the expense of peer approval.

o They'll begin to develop skills beyond those required to do the job they're presently assigned to, because they will see potential for themselves.

o They'll remove themselves from the ranks of middle managers who complain of being oversupervised or undersupervised.

Management that apes the old games of "Simon says . . ." or "Mother, may I . . ." is not only old hat but counterproductive. Of course, managers have to direct work, and at times that direction has to be very specific and people have to be closely supervised. And, too, there are times when managers have to cut people loose to do the best they can with the problems before them. However, good delegators never get a reputation for being "Simon" or "Mother"; they just get a reputation for being *good bosses.*

Good bosses often get pleasant bonuses when they delegate effectively. They may not take the form of checks from the front office, but they will come as freely offered ideas from subordinates who feel comfortable making suggestions. You've probably noticed that there's an interesting correlation between managers who delegate and managers who are open to new ideas. It works both ways—for the good of the manager as well as for the good of the subordinates and the company.

8

She Got the Biggest Piece,
But You Got the Frosting

We can present all kinds of wise sayings and clichés like, "Man does not live by bread alone," "Money isn't everything," "You can't take it with you," "Satisfaction is its own reward," and the scars of inequities still remain. *What* and *how* people are rewarded for their time, skill, and effort *are* important.

I have had conversations with executives who seem to believe that once a union contract has been negotiated, the problems of pay and benefits have been resolved until the contract is reopened. And they apply that kind of thinking beyond the ranks of the represented workers; they believe that management pay and benefits are likewise neatly established and properly administered. Sometimes. Not always.

I have also had conversations with managers—not all from the same company or the same industry—who were seriously contemplating forming management unions. What is really disconcerting about this is that these are people who, earlier in their careers, would have rejected the idea out of hand. When the issue is pursued with these managers, they don't place the blame on their companies' salary administration department but on their own managers, who appear to operate in a cavalier manner *within* the established policies. In fact, they indicate that the inequities they observe are peculiarly middle management problems.

If we take as an example a commonly used grade/salary-range

system—jobs ranked, let's say, from grade one to grade 20, with the lower grades assigned to clerical and the higher grades assigned to executive personnel—snap logic would say that the system takes care of the problem. What we know is that, in most systems, pay ranges of given grades overlap with the contiguous grades, and rightly so. A grade 14 job will have its feet in the upper reaches of a grade 13, and its head will be in the lower reaches of a grade 15. Nothing to it. Assign the grade, and the pay will take care of itself. Maybe.

Managers can play with other managers' pay plans in a number of ways—by rewriting job descriptions to justify a higher grade, for example. If I like Jack particularly well, I can juggle an extra grade for him. It may take some time, but I can beat the salary administrator at his or her own game. Or I can always give Jack the maximum merit increase and make the other increases lower so that the company average is maintained. The list of tricks could go on and on. Now it's entirely possible that Jack deserves all this. It's also an even bet that others may not think so.

The naive think that salary policies are as immutable as the law of gravity; the crafty look on them as a challenge to be conquered. But the real issue is the perception people have of their proper rewards as being the result of what services they perform. And this is where good management takes special care to communicate and administer pay and benefits on an individual basis. If I have confidence in my boss, I feel that what I am getting for what I am doing is proper and in line with what others are getting. Managers have to earn that kind of confidence by their actions and their explanations.

A good friend of mine works for a major corporation. He resigned from a sales management position and went back to selling, because, as he put it, "I couldn't afford the privilege." When I told my friend that it's not uncommon in sales organizations for individual sales representatives to make more money that their managers, he countered with this: "Selling does involve some elements of risk. Selling is totally based on productivity—you either make it or you don't. I don't deny the sales rep one cent. But more often than not, the sales manager gives immediate support to the sales representative, sometimes travels with him or her and helps wrap up certain big deals, supervises the paperwork and the back-up . . . and never figures in the success story. But that's not all. The *manager* not only *makes* less but has to *spend* more; the position carries with it the obligations of club memberships and charity donations and an endless number of costly little things that whittle away at what you do earn."

Another friend told me a different story, but indicating similar inequities. In a corporate reorganization, he had been assigned larger responsibilities. Ironically, he was awarded the very job he had wanted several years earlier but never got; he had been promoted away from the department into another job. Now he was called back and was delighted to return. The work was satisfying, the environment was exciting, and the pay and benefits were in line with his expectations.

Because this executive was just a few years away from retirement, he set about finding someone who could be groomed to take his place. What he discovered was that the company was willing to pay the apprentice *journeyman* wages: the same as his! "It's the law of the market that prevails," he was told. Somehow, I believe he thought it was more like the law of the jungle.

I tried to give my friend some solace by describing other situations, like the company that took all its executives and upper-level managers off the cost-of-living system and reinstated a bonus plan. At first blush, that made sense—rewards would flow to the deserving. But market conditions wiped out profitability, and no bonuses were forthcoming. Meanwhile, *everyone else* raked in the COLA money, because inflation had spiraled. Middle managers found themselves supervising subordinates who made more money than they did! My friend's comment was terse: "That's bad policy, but I'm talking about bad practice!"

Policy *or* practice, management has to be concerned about equitable payment of people. Unions work full time at securing equitable payment. Sit in on a few negotiating sessions, as I have, and you'll discover that watchdogs really do exist. Argue both sides of the union question, agree or disagree with strategies and tactics, but you have to admit that nothing much gets overlooked. And the overlooked is what seems to flourish in many middle management situations.

What about merit increases? They should resolve the issue, shouldn't they? They not only don't resolve it but often irritate it. Two quite opposite practices prevail: Some managers cop out and give everyone a little annual boost, deserved or not; other managers take care of a few and ignore the rest. The first manager argues that everyone expects something each year, and the other says, "I'll do what I very well please."

Douglas McGregor, in his last book, *The Professional Manager,*[*] discussed the subject of managerial power. Within the power category is the control of extrinsic rewards and punishments. He described a situation in which he queried middle and lower management groups about the extent to which they felt salary increases were related to successful effort. The response was most often "a cynical smile." He also reported a study conducted by Rensis Likert on employees who were at the top of their salary brackets but not promotable. When they received praise for good work, they were annoyed rather than pleased. So it goes. Despite a lot of fine study, thought, and writing about the idea that money is not a motivator, it still remains a powerful attitude influencer.

Frederick Herzberg put it correctly. He listed money and other items of compensation and benefits as dissatisfiers. We are pleased to be paid, but if we sense any inequity about the payment, we are quick to criticize—regardless of how munificent the arrangement may be. The more I discuss this matter with middle managers, the more convinced I am that Herzberg was right, and that many present-day managers are wrong. There is bound to be a built-in flaw in nearly every compensation system, but poor administration

* New York: McGraw-Hill, 1967.

of that system makes it appear even worse. It's something every manager should guard against.

That also applies to a lot of other managerial perquisites. If you have ever paid close attention to inner-office conflicts, you must have noticed how jealous people become over physical arrangements—offices and furniture, who has a secretary and who doesn't, and so on. It has little to do with function, but a lot to do with interpersonal relationships and attitudes.

I have usually laughed at these petty jealousies, probably because I have nearly always been satisfied with my own work stations. I recall my first brush with the problem years ago. I was at General Electric and not yet familiar with the workings of big-league management. Our group was moved from one building to another, and although there were partitions stacked against the wall, they had not yet been put in place. We inquired when the work would be finished so that we could settle in and get down to business. We were told that before the work could be done, an already erected wall had to be torn down, new pilasters ordered, and a replotting of the area completed. The real problem, it turned out, was that if the offices were built without such reconstruction, my office would be one foot shorter than that of another supervisor. I went to the executive in charge and told him it didn't make any difference to either of us. The offices were put in place the next day, and we got along very nicely. Company policy, in this case, had guarded against a possible cause of jealousy.

Some years later, I was employed by a very large training and promotion agency. Offices, at best, were not very attractive, and many of them were inside units with no natural light. I occupied one of those little boxes for several months. Then one day I was invited to move to another office—with a *window!* That pleased me, but how it annoyed others who had been with the shop much longer. I took the new office, but I felt for them.

My last office in a corporate setting was quite pleasant. It was in a new building, had a nicely draped window wall that looked out onto a grassy and tree-lined patio, and was well furnished—desk, bookcases, chairs for visitors, and attractive pictures on the wall. I thought I was king of the hill until my son took me to *his* office in a Chicago suburb some months later. He had *two* glass walls, a superb view of Lake Michigan, a couch, and a coffee table. Discrimination! Young executives get it all!

We smile at these things, call them petty and unimportant, but they do impact mightily on some individuals. Not everyone can have the top grade or the top pay, and not everyone can have the corner office on the view-side of the building. But it's important that every manager who manages other managers be conscious of these concerns and do two things:

1. Administer existing policy as equitably as possible.
2. Communicate differences and be prepared to defend them.

We must eliminate managerial judgments like these:

- Let's pass over Dan's raise this time. His wife is working, and they don't need the money.
- Sure Charlie deserves the promotion, but we have this new guy who needs some seasoning, and that spot would be just great for him. Charlie will wait.
- So what if the trainee makes more than Margaret does? He's going to report to her only for the balance of the year. We'll get around to Margaret later.
- I know Jerry doesn't deserve a reserved parking space, but he's in and out of the building a lot.
- Send a group of people out on identical trips, and Mac's expenses will always be $25 higher than anyone else's. Oh, well, I'd rather get cheated than listen to him gripe.
- That's right. Shelley has a higher grade than Marie, but unless she kicks about it, I'm not going to make any office changes.

We are talking here about two different but very closely related things—equitable treatment and adequate communication. They are equal and opposite sides of the same coin. Policies generally begin with a sense of fairness. They deteriorate with bad handling and poor communications.

Let's consider first the practice and the policy that is aimed at equitable treatment. Most compensation programs are based on the skill, care, effort, and responsibility involved in the job. Most well-structured systems involve identifiable grades or levels of compensation—ostensibly tied to the job evaluation factors just named. On paper, this can look very impressive. In practice, it can become a mare's nest. So much of the administration of the program rests on the individual manager that, equitable as the system may appear to be, inequities can abound within it.

There are four basic considerations to look at:

1. The grade itself.
2. The point within that grade at which a person is placed at the time of original assignment.
3. Time in grade.
4. Merit increases.

We might regard the establishment of the grade, using the job description as its basis, as reasonably sacrosanct. After all, didn't someone study the grade and put a price tag on the job? Of course, but consider this commonly told story:

Mike is a department manager. He has six supervisors reporting to him. Four of those supervisors do pretty much the same thing and are paid the same grade, with the variables of time in grade and merit applied. The other two supervisors, because of the unique character of their work, are a grade higher. One of the higher-rated supervisors retires. In the course of attempting to fill the vacancy, the other supervisors are considered but rejected for various reasons. So far, no real flaw in the program.

Mike desperately needs someone in that position. In considering candidates, he recalls Peggy, who used to work in the section and was especially talented, but who was lured away to another department on a promotion. She would be an excellent candidate. He discovers, however, that she already has an equivalent grade in the other department. To get her back would mean regrading the job here. By adding a few elements to the job description—none of which is either new or essential—Mike convinces the salary administrator that the job is bigger than it was before.

To top it off, he hires Peggy in on the high side of the salary spread. She comes into the job, is paid more than her experienced counterpart, and will be less productive until she learns the ropes. But the inequity doesn't stop there. When merit increases are granted and when general increases are applied, the differential grows geometrically. Once ahead, always ahead.

This is the sort of thing that currently annoys many middle managers. They find themselves at midcareer earning no more than raw recruits from college campuses. They find themselves in secondary roles, while rotating-assignment people get top spots for "seasoning." They begin to discover that *doing* a good job may be less well rewarded than *seeking* a good job: Don't offer Harry the promotion, because he's too valuable where he is. And age discrimination plays a role, too: If Warren doesn't get the promotion, he won't quit anyhow, because he has too much to lose in pension and benefits.

To be completely fair, we also have to look at the other side of this problem. In most business organizations, there are some older people who plug up opportunities because they are where they want to be and feel perfectly justified in resting on their oars. Sinecures exist all over industry. This points up a flaw in the managers rather than in the system, however. As we admitted earlier, some middle management problems are created by middle managers themselves. By ignoring realities, by taking the easy way out, by not wanting to stir up the animal, many managers have allowed inequities to creep into otherwise equitable systems.

I can never claim to have solved this problem during my own managerial career, but I tried to address it whenever I could. On several occasions, I was forced to absorb personnel from other departments and divisions that were faced with "head-count reductions." Company policy allowed me to cut the grades, but not the pay. That meant that the transferee lost certain perquisites yet didn't suffer at the pay window. On the surface, that was a generous position for the company to take, but it had a number of detrimental side effects.

Here were people earning more than their counterparts for doing the very same job. In one case that I recall, the transferee made more than I did (undoubtedly that instance sparked my sensitivity to this particular inequity). It was patently unfair, especially when general increases were granted, because when you add 5 percent to a 20 percent overpayment, you have actually granted a 6 percent increase. Do that often enough and see where it will get you! My avenue of correction lay solely in the awarding of merit increases: I refused to do it. That brought on the laments and explanations, but it had to be done.

And that brings us to the second vital area of any workable compensation program—communicating it. Unless people actually know and understand the system and how you apply it, even perfectly equitable administration loses value. The important thing about communications in this area is that the manager should be in full control of it. That isn't always the case, although it should be.

Although managers keep salary records securely locked in their desks or files, and although discussions with employees regarding salary and benefits are carried on behind closed doors, it's amazing how much some people know about other people's business. One obvious leak is the secretarial grapevine. It's important that a secretary be cautioned against revealing information to others. But even with that leak plugged securely, information does seem to get around. Some of it is due to the indiscretions of middle managers themselves.

You've probably experienced a situation such as this: I was announcing a 3 percent general increase to my supervisors. (That was back when 3 percent seemed to mean something.) One of the members of the group—a man known more for his energy and enthusiasm than for his ability to keep a secret—did some quick calculations on the back of an envelope and exclaimed, "Oh, boy! That's over 600 bucks. It'll sure come in handy!" You could see the icy glances darting in all directions. Unfortunately, several of his peers wouldn't get that much, and the cover was blown! Here was one of those situations described earlier, in which the employee had been transferred in at a higher rate, then given general increases and deserved merit increases that multiplied one upon the other. There were reasons for the differences, but those who earned less didn't care to hear those reasons. In a private session later on, the employee came to understand that salary was confidential, a matter for the individual and me. *We* might agree he was properly compensated, but did others?

Here are some guidelines for communicating pay and benefit information to managers:

• Policy changes and general information should be given to managers first. They should be directed to communicate the same information immediately to their work groups.

• Discussions of individual salary and benefit matters should be held privately, with the added caution that such information is to be kept private.

• Managers whose pay and benefits rise above those of others holding similar rank should be told that their rewards have been earned and deserved.

• Managers whose pay and benefits fall below those of others holding similar rank should know that they have a long way to go before they can reach the highest levels of rewards. This is a difficult thing to do, incidentally, and many managers fail to face up to the responsibility. Poor performers tend to be tolerated, seldom counseled. By the time it begins to show up in the pay check, it's often too late.

• When perquisites go with a salary grade, grant them immediately. If that means an improved office, see to it that an improved office is made available.

• Counsel achievers on their behavior and attitude toward those who have not been so successful. The person whose grade gives him or her a reserved parking space, for instance, should use it to park a car, not to brag about.

• If corporate policies vary for different pay grades, communicate the differences. Expense account policies often differ—higher-level managers are privileged, let's say, to take a staff member to lunch, while that staff member cannot take one of his or her subordinates to lunch. Open communication at an early stage saves misunderstandings later on.

• Be a communications example to subordinates. Encourage them to be equally open and informative.

• If inequities seem to be the result of policy, take the matter up with your manager. Communications upward are important, too. You may see things awry at your level that aren't evident at your manager's.

• If the aforementioned inequity has become a matter of discussion among your own staff, be sure they know what has been done to correct it or, if it is not being corrected, why.

• Be open to an upward flow of ideas on this subject. It is not simple, nor is it comfortable, to deal with feelings, but it should be done. Begin with the point of view that the person who comes to you with a complaint is serious and deserving of an audience.

• Maintain a careful policy of dealing within the corporate structure and organizational lines. Don't bypass one of your managers or supervisors by going into these matters below his or her level.

When you deal equitably and openly with people in your organization, you do the following things for your subordinates:

○ You free them up to move ahead on the job without the nagging feeling that they're not well cared for.

○ You give them the idea that performance will curry more favor than politicking will.

○ You set an example for them to carry to the next lower level. The farther the example travels, the more productive the work group will be.

And you pick up a few worthwhile benefits, too:

○ You put an end to a lot of petty bickering and avoid wasting a lot of time explaining your way out of corners.

○ You build credibility with your immediate subordinates that should, inevitably, trickle down through the whole organization.
○ You earn from your superiors a reputation for having things well in hand.
○ Your entire organization will address itself to the goals established for it. Discontented people have a splended talent for withholding effort when they want to. Let your management be additive rather than subtractive.

The behavioral scientists—and I count myself only an adherent and a practitioner of their point of view—focus most of their attention on motivation at levels higher than mere financial incentives and other tangible rewards. Achievement, the self-esteem that accrues from recognized performance, the social benefits—all are important. But let people feel that they are not being treated fairly and in accordance with some traditionally acceptable standards applied equally to them and to others, and you have a problem on your hands. Man assuredly does not live by bread alone, but cut him a smaller slice of the loaf than he thinks he deserves, and you'll surely hear about it!

9

Why Is the Job Described One Way and the Performance Measured Another?

In the foregoing chapter, we explored the matter of equitable treatment in managerial ranks. That involved a cursory look at job descriptions and pay grades. It also involved some brief commentary on the communications process as it supports the concept of equal treatment. Both topics deserve additional consideration.

What annoys many middle managers is the fact that they often see little relationship between what the job is described as being, the grade that's assigned to it, and the effect performance has on promotions and additional pay and benefits. It's little wonder that they are perplexed: The entire matter is seldom handled with the precision with which it is described in the corporate policy manual. What the people in the personnel department believe is happening and what *really* is going on may be two very different things.

When you were first hired into a supervisory role, you were undoubtedly handed a piece of paper called a job description. If you were promoted into that position from the ranks, you were impressed with the idea that your management was well organized and that your job, and presumably the jobs of others, was clearly and crisply spelled out. If you came into supervision straight out of college, you thought that what the professor in Management 101 said was true: Business operates by the book. It didn't take you long, however, to discover that all you read on that piece of paper wasn't necessarily so. As one of my business colleagues once said,

"The most accurate item on my job description is the last-line disclaimer—*and to perform other duties as may be assigned.*"

However necessary that "last-line disclaimer" may seem to be to many managers, it ultimately is the great management cop-out. You see, it does a number of important things for the manager who is not willing to make an initial commitment or maintain a responsible degree of control:

○ It saves rewriting the job description as the work mix changes.
○ It puts the manager in control on a day-to-day basis.
○ It keeps the manager from being painted into a corner on performance appraisals and job evaluations.
○ It keeps the employee wondering what his or her responsibilities are and, thus, utterly dependent upon orders from the manager.

That's bad management. True, but there is a lot of it, so we should face up to it. Many managers may not intend to operate that way, but it does happen that many job descriptions in today's business environment are outdated, poorly constructed, and inadequately used. Whoever must assume the ultimate blame, it remains the up-close concern of *any* manager at *any* level to make sure that it doesn't affect his or her immediate subordinates. You see, it really doesn't make much difference whether corporate practice is inadequate and/or poorly monitored; the individual manager can make the job description system operate properly within his or her immediate range of control.

Ideally, job descriptions are the creation of the manager in whose department those jobs are performed. Again, ideally, the work of the manager is reviewed by the manager one level above and by people in the personnel department who may have special training and insight into the composition of such an instrument. And that may happen in many instances, particularly when a new department is formed or a major reorganization takes place. In practice, however, the process usually takes a different shape. A manager moves into a department post, takes the organization and the individual jobs assigned to it, and lets it be. The manager's intent may be to make changes . . . later. Later may become seldom or never.

To continue is easier than to create: "Let's just see how this works out before tampering with a functioning entity." Sometimes that approach makes very good sense, because who is to say that one's predecessor necessarily did things poorly? But you've been through this, as I have; the problems that beset the chair I'm sitting in take up so much of my time that I don't get a moment to think about the chairs that surround me. As weeks turn to months, and months turn to years, the importance of reviewing and redoing job descriptions seems to dwindle. Letting a job description get out of date is that simple and that explainable.

But it isn't defensible. I have seen situations where managers go over an individual's existing job description only to hear, "I know that's in my description, but in reality Wally takes care of that. You see, he has all those records, and when he pulls his report on production volume together, he also makes out the inventory report. Besides, it's all computerized, anyhow. I get the printout, but I don't generate it." The responsible manager promptly makes the change in both descriptions. The less responsible manager says, "I'll make that change when I redo the job descriptions." It doesn't get done.

In an environment such as was just described, it's simple for the idler to pass off responsibilities on the poor person who is willing to accept them. It's also simple for the aggressive manager to take on responsibilities that don't belong to him or her; gather enough of them and bring the matter to the boss's attention, and you can get your job regraded and up you go. It happens every day to someone's gain and to someone's loss. The practice flourishes best in environments that are poorly disciplined. It can even happen that the slippage in monitoring job descriptions can work to the boss's detriment. The usurper gathers the control and manages from below. Have you ever seen a manager replaced by one of his or her subordinates—fire one and promote the other? Guess how that happened.

The role of the impartial third party—personnel—is vital in keeping things on track. Here again, many managers work hard at holding personnel or organization people at arm's length. "If I start working up new job descriptions, those guys will get to poking around, and I'm likely to be told I can't do what I want. Might even lose grades." But such external groups see the job descriptions and organization charts of many departments side by side. That precludes or diminishes duplication and overlap. And who knows? Maybe it could work in your favor to have your descriptions compared to others.

Each manager or supervisor should have his or her own job description. That's true, regardless of company policy. It's only fair to know *what* you're expected to do; what responsibilities and relationships are to be maintained; and what level of authority you have in such areas as delegation, authorization of expenditures, hiring and firing of employees, approving privileges, pay raises, promotions, and so forth. I'd take that one step further: Every member of a manager's staff should be able to see where his or her job description varies, overlaps, joins, or conflicts with the job descriptions of peers. That not only helps them know what they *should* be doing but also tells them what they *should not* be doing. Let the boundaries be official, and let them be clearly understood.

Unlike the discussion of salary, which must be private, the discussion of work assignments and responsibility should be staffwide. If I have Sam, Ethel, Jack, and Jill all doing essentially the same things in 90 percent of their workloads, I should be open in pointing out where the 10 percent difference lies. All they have to do is look around them to know that each member of the group has some special area of activity and responsibility. They should know that this is a matter of design, not happenstance. It should be a thing that is discussed, explained, and approved, not just gossiped about. If members of the group feel that the setup is not to their liking, that can be a matter of private conversation. Sometimes we manage groups, and sometimes we manage individuals. Good managers know the difference.

I once inherited a badly formed work group. I couldn't blame it on my manager, because he had preceded me in his position by only a month or so. He explained that he had not made changes, even though changes were indicated, simply because he wanted his new key staff to be party to the reorganization. He was right, and I appreciated the consideration. It could have been otherwise, and I might have suffered for a long time with an arrangement I couldn't work with. One of the difficulties that came with the opportunity, however, was the necessity of rewriting all job descriptions. We reviewed the files, found the old descriptions, discovered that they were not suitable to our new view of how the department should operate, and decided to start back at square one. That's where the fun began.

I called in those key people for whom I had appointments in mind. They were the individuals with experience and professional credentials who were the more obvious candidates for supervisory posts. Indeed, certain of them were at that moment handling many of the supervisory functions necessary to the operation, even though they carried no titles. I asked each, in turn, to come in with his or her current job description. To my surprise, nobody could come up with one. Their former manager had never seen fit to issue them, or if he had, little importance was attached to the matter.

The inquiry went like this: What do you *now* do? What do you think you *should* be doing? What do you think *needs* to be done that isn't being done? Of all the things we've talked about, what would you *like* to do most? What *could* you do best? It was a risky business, but how else would one go about charting new territory?

Needless to say, not everyone got his or her wish. In some cases, the results of the interviews precluded particular appointments. But a combination of what we learned and what we already had in mind helped bring a new organization into focus and new job descriptions into line. The net result was an organization that was 90 percent new. It was also an organization that wasn't entirely happy, because some individuals lost responsibilities they liked, took on ones they didn't like, and had to replace old habits with new ones. There was also that undercurrent of, "I work harder than he does." Until people work *with* people, it can hardly be called an organization. Individuals at work . . . yes. Individuals working together . . . no.

The rearrangement of the workload applied to a number of the supervisory positions. Here again, some lost responsibilities, while others gained them. Until I caught on to the fact that part of their discomfort stemmed from their unawareness of the specifics of the *other* supervisory responsibilities, I regarded the entire climate as a malaise just short of a quiet mutiny. What required repair was a communications problem, and the repair was relatively simple: Call the staff together and show them the elements of responsibility side by side. To say that worked perfectly would be an overstatement, but it did work well. In some cases, we made accommodating adjustments. In other cases, we stood fast and defended the plan. The organization began to pull together.

The point of all this is that people in an organization are not like tiles on a wall. They don't just fit together, they *hinge* together. People not only have to know what their individual responsibilities are, but they also have to see how they interface with others. *Unless* that happens, the managerial role is a difficult one. *Until* that happens, organization charts and job descriptions are just so much corporate wallpaper. When a job description comes alive and stays alive, it begins to work for the individual holding that position, the manager to whom he or she is responsible, and the company that pays for the services of both.

Managers must make job descriptions come alive on the employee's first encounter with them. To hand an individual a job description and go over it hurriedly is a mistake. That gives the impression that it is something to be scanned quickly and filed—and forgotten in some instances. You may not want to treat such material with absolute reverence, but neither can you treat it as routine prose—a mere formality. On that piece of paper is the direction required for satisfactory achievement. Inherent in its presentation is the fact that it will serve as the yardstick for measuring what is satisfactory. Unless that is known up front, don't expect too much from it later on.

It is the unusual organization that doesn't undergo change in the course of time. Here's a new project . . . give it to Shirley. This is one of those assignments that comes up from time to time and doesn't really belong to the department's charter . . . Murphy can handle it. There is no question that some assignments are temporary or unexpected, and we shouldn't feel obliged to rewrite a job description each time a minor specialty task comes on stream. But we have to recognize one important thing: While Shirley is doing the new project, and while Murphy is getting that little matter attended to, they can't spend the time and effort they would like to be spending on their own *assigned* jobs. And what if specialty projects like that keep coming to the department? Like thieves in the night, they creep into the picture, and what was once temporary becomes permanent. When that happens, the job description begins to look like last year's styles—a little out of place in fine company!

The whole purpose of an organization chart and job descriptions, of course, is to bring about suitable performance that ultimately translates into departmental, divisional, and corporate success. More to the point, however, is that it translates into individual success and the much-needed sense of personal accomplishment. That's a complaint of many middle managers: They claim their errors get instant recognition, but their achievements go unsung. Now, how in the world can that happen when we have annual performance reviews?

I've received performance reviews, and I've given them. I've noticed that there's a contagion of sorts when it comes to performance reviews—*get* good ones, and you'll *conduct* good ones. That's another reason why middle managers have to be careful about playing follow-the-leader. Do follow if the leader does things well, but don't follow if he or she doesn't. The place to begin management reform is in your own office, talking to your own subordinates about their performances. Do it well, and you will have set a pattern for them to do it well, too.

Most companies with which I have had any substantial contact through direct employment or extended consultation make *annual* performance reviews a rite. The best counseling experience I ever had, however, was with trainees with whom quarterly reviews were required. The annual review spans too long a period and focuses too much attention on the formality. My recommendation would be for reviews to be held at least semiannually, with the annual review keyed to the awarding of merit increases. But even more helpful than that would be to put a tickler note on the calendar to bring subordinates in every two or three months on a talk-it-over basis and to maintain an ongoing list of items worth commenting on pro and con.

Managers can take a tip on that from professional football coaches. Watch them on television. The player who makes an exceptional play not only hears about it from the crowd but gets a nod, a pat, or a word of congratulations right on the spot. Let him make a blunder, and he'll hear about that, too. The secret is in the immediacy of the comment. If more managers would provide feedback on a regular basis, the annual performance review could be put on the shelf. It's because many managers must be *forced* to comment favorably or criticize constructively that appraisals had to be ritualized.

That doesn't mean that the annual review has no merit. It has great merit, because it helps create a record, and it does assure that at least minimal contact has been made. However, when more frequent and less formal performance discussions are held, the rigidity and the awesome importance of the annual review fade. Also, interim corrections forestall continuing error and accelerate correct performance. That's what management is about—*getting* performance, not simply measuring it.

Here are some guidelines for developing the kind of job descriptions that can serve as a truly effective basis for performance appraisal:

* Study good job description models. You'll find they all have a common format: title, function, responsibilities, authority, relationships. Go beyond that and pay attention to the language. Simple is better than legalese.

* Study the job. What needs to be done is the vital factor. When it comes to writing the responsibilities section, be sure to express responsibilities in terms of *what* to do, not *how* to do it.

* Study the individual assigned or to be assigned. Although jobs remain and people come and go, there's no sense in creating a job that can't be done by the person holding it.

* Talk to people. Your manager can provide good counsel. So can the incumbent. So can managers and supervisors who occupy positions with which the job will interface.

* Write it. Pull out the responsibilities section so that it can be used to compare this job with other jobs in the organization.

* Discuss it with the person assigned. Make sure there is a mutual understanding about responsibilities and accountabilities. Take time in this discussion session: Confirm understanding and focus attention on the job description as the basis for performance appraisal.

Most corporate performance appraisal forms bear no similarity to the job description. Little wonder why some middle managers lament that they are assigned duties to perform but are reviewed on the basis of personality, interpersonal relationships, responsiveness—almost never on the basis of *specific, job-related* performance. Oh, it's there, but it has no definite connection to the particulars of the job description. And equally distressing is the fact that managers who review performance with lower-level managers and supervisors seldom attempt to establish that connection.

I would cite one exception: Early in managerial careers, performance appraisals do seem to come more frequently and have more meaning. The newly appointed supervisor or manager comes under the scrutiny of his or her boss in a way that the "settled-in" manager doesn't. There may be a number of valid reasons for this—the manager's concern about having made a good selection, an honest attempt to bring about the best performance possible, a proper effort to correct poor performance or inappropriate behavior. I would propose one more reason: The difference in age, experience, position, and power between the manager and his or her apprentice creates a psychological comfort factor in the downward relationship. The manager says: "I can tell this kid, and he'll listen. He has a lot to learn, and he knows it." It's simply a case of advantage and leverage.

So in a performance appraisal between the new hire and the old hand, there's a parent/child or teacher/learner relationship. One believes he or she has the license to give instruction, and the other feels obligated to receive it. But what does a manager do with a seasoned subordinate who has a lot of tenure in the position, keeps his or her head down, and does a satisfactory job? The assumption is that old Bill knows the job like the back of his hand, stays out of trouble, remains reliable, and is at the top of the pay grade, so what is there to say to Bill? Just keep the appraisal marks above average, spend three minutes telling him he's a good guy, and let it go at that.

And there's the rub! Many middle managers who earlier in their careers received a lot of attention from their bosses now feel that their boss doesn't notice, doesn't care, and isn't looking after their interests. That may not be the case, but it appears to be so. I've even had some managers tell me: "I could put up with constructive criticism better than with anonymity. If I'm doing well, I'd like to know how well I'm doing. If I'm doing something that keeps me from making more money or getting a promotion, I'd like to know that, too. This once-a-year 'Keep it up, Joe' is damned little satisfaction."

So, in the final analysis, what about performance appraisals? Are they worth anything at all? Are they too perfunctory, too organizational or institutional in character? The answer is that they *are* worth something and that they can and should be kept vital through proper handling by the manager. Here are some thoughts about the preparation and administration of performance appraisals:

• Don't regard appraisals as just a once-a-year activity. Take the initiative to have periodic sit-down conversations on specific performance factors with each manager or supervisor in your organization.

• Keep a log of such conversations. As important as the substance of the discussions is their frequency.

• If the corporate appraisal form is designed with a quick checklist, delay scoring by the numbers until you have written your comments on specific performance factors. Then go back and fill in the spaces for self-confidence, integrity, attitude, and so forth.

• Keep side notes—substantive information not called for on the appraisal form. This provides you with talking paper and may help you defend a point of view. Include times, dates, places. The more specific, the more terrific.

• Allocate sufficient time for individual conferences with members of your staff. Never let it appear that today is appraisal day at the old mill.

• When you invite your subordinate in for the conference, specify in the invitation that this is to be an appraisal discussion. He or she may want to bring along materials to support a point of view.

• Put your subordinate at ease. In doing so, however, don't go overboard and make it appear that this is just a casual affair; on the other hand, don't make it appear as though this is the day of final judgment, either.

• Attempt to separate the personal from the measurable elements as much as possible. Use the job description.

• Read your comments.

• Seek responses.

• In the case of a critical observation, ask if the interviewee can see how you arrived at the criticism.

• In the case of a compliment, make it sincere and don't attempt to qualify it.

- In the event of wholly satisfactory performance, express hope that it will continue that way.
- In the event of unsatisfactory performance, offer help in correcting the situation. Always leave the subordinate with the feeling that he or she can turn the low grade into a high one with specified behavior.
- Keep the entire conversation private in every way. That means no postconference idle chatter.

In the whole matter of what is *expected* of an individual and how that individual *fulfills* the expectations, we are dealing with perceptions and feelings. I may not be performing well but think I am. I may be performing well, but you haven't noticed. I may be comparing myself to someone else who, in my opinion, doesn't work as hard or accomplish as much as I do. Performance appraisals must be done with solid observations and a lot of impartiality. And they have to be done without lies. Only the manager can set the appropriate tone that will filter down through his or her organization.

When you build job descriptions that say something and base your evaluations on what those job descriptions say, you've gone a long way toward generating good performance in your subordinates. Here's what it does for them:

- It gives them a feeling of worth.
- It makes them believe that you care, and that you have defined the difference between good and poor performance and will appraise them accordingly.
- It gives them an opportunity to point out their own inadequacies and insecurities as well as the built-in organizational obstacles to their performance.
- It marks the point of a new beginning—something we all need once in a while.

And you profit, too:

- You build a reputation as a performance-oriented manager.
- You put an end to feelings that you don't notice or don't care.

o You get the work you require and the respect you deserve.
o You become an example for your subordinates—especially if you advise them to take the same care with their work groups as you have taken with them.

A fellow manager once jokingly said to me that when performance appraisal time came along, it was the one time in the year he felt like God. I asked him whether it was when he gave appraisals or received them. He didn't think that was funny.

Appraisals are serious business. They should be considered an ongoing responsibility of every manager. That's true of relationships with all employees, but it's particularly true with managers. Middle managers really are in the middle. They give and receive. They know the difference . . . and make a difference.

10

I Know You Folks Are Busy, But This Is Really Important

As I queried middle managers about their many discontents, they repeatedly came up with responses that are best summarized by, "My boss sees the work I do as necessary but not so vital that it can't be interrupted or put off." When asked to refine that complaint, the list of things that interrupt the central role of the subordinate manager included tasks like running errands, doing favors, working at menial chores, attending superfluous meetings, handling unplanned activities, and other similar time wasters. The war stories were fantastic.

There was the case of the president of a small company who conducted an annual press conference, complete with entertainment and refreshments ad infinitum. It was a gala affair, always held in conjunction with a community activity that drew a lot of press people in, and the company capitalized on a readily available audience. Guess who the bartenders were? Vice-presidents and department managers had aprons on and were up to their elbows in ice cubes and lemon peel. It wasn't a matter of expense; the budget was seemingly unlimited. It wasn't a matter of putting managers into a position of availability for conversation; they were too busy to talk. It was the top man's annual demonstration of who ran the show. He thought he was being very funny when he said, "It's the one time each year when I know where they are and can be certain they're doing something constructive."

Then there was the story of the manager who was called upon frequently by visitors, many of whom flew in and out the same day. His supervisory staff used to keep score in one of the offices regarding which of them was called upon most often to drive the visitors back to the airport. "These are important people," the boss would say. "They shouldn't have to take a cab."

And the story about the manager whose boss was building a new home. "Run out and see how they're coming along. And also call the plumber to make sure of. . . ." It started as a favor and ended up as an assignment. Or the story about the department that literally shut down for two days so that its managers and supervisors could run the local charity golf tournament. The list goes on and on—cab driving, baby-sitting, ticket taking, tour guiding, and many other nonbusiness, nonsupervisory activities. Whether they are based on expediency or whim, such practices add up to an inefficient use of human resources and an abuse of managerial privilege.

Granted, much of this is mere thoughtlessness. In retrospect, I declare myself guilty of doing many of the things I criticize today. More than once have I handed my car keys to one of the department supervisors and said, "Will you run Jack over to the hotel? I have a dozen things to do before the end of the day." The inference, of course, was that *I* was busy; my subordinate wasn't. *My* work was important; the subordinate's wasn't.

What is strange about this is that I was always more conscious of the improper assignment of personnel when it involved someone else's department. Periodically, my work took me to regional or zone sales offices. The managers there would always offer to have someone pick me up at the airport. At times I would accept the invitation, but many times I refused, saying, "Your guys are too busy. I'll just grab a cab." What is the old saying? A carpenter's house is always in need of repair?

Whether it's a case of a superior's borrowing your secretary to fill in for the lobby receptionist for a day, or having you cancel long-made plans for some on-the-spot chore that strikes his or her fancy, you find yourself in that impasse where it's wrong to say yes, but it's suicide to say no. Or is it? Perhaps the problem in this regard is that too many managers—throughout their careers—become acclimated to giving in and being given in to. That is a classic weakness of highly directive management, a subject we'll cover later in this book.

Essentially, three problems are afoot in this kind of situation:

o A misdirected use of power coupled with a lack of appreciation of the importance of functions under one's control.
o A failure to apply principles of time management not only to oneself but to others.
o A flawed communications process up, down, and across the organization.

The next time you invite someone to "come right down" to your office, consider what is happening. The next time you hand out some task that looks like a personal errand, consider the consequences. And the next time you set dates without clearing them with those who are affected, consider the outcome. Reverse those situations, and the picture is clear: You don't like it, so neither should the people on whom you heap such inconveniences.

In a practical sense, we must admit that rank and priorities have to have a reasonable match. The manager above must have justifiable freedom to intervene and interrupt processes controlled by the manager below. We don't shut down the plant because the sweeper shows up to clean it, and neither do we cancel the training program to make plans for the company picnic. We do shut down a line that's producing bad pieces, and we do require change in schedules that are not in the best interest of the business. Judgment and power have to go down the same road—together. Sometimes they don't. But there are ways to see that they do.

Consider for a moment the principles of time management. Merrill Douglass* does a neat job of categorizing activities and

* *Manage Your Time, Manage Your Work, Manage Your Life* (New York; AMA-COM, 1980).

putting priorities on them. Whatever he writes, wherever he speaks, he lists these classifications:

Important *and* urgent.
Important, *not* urgent.
Urgent, *not* important.
Neither urgent *nor* important.

As managers, we have to be able to make those four distinctions. The annoyance factors and war stories listed above all hinge on those priorities—or the misplacement of them. It would be worthwhile at this point to refresh our memories regarding the differences.

You're going to have a meeting of your field managers. They're coming in from all corners of the country. Plans and arrangements have been carefully made, and everything is coming off according to plan, when you get a telephone call from the speaker who is scheduled to be the cornerstone of the program. He is flat on his back in bed and under doctor's orders to stay that way. The meeting begins in two days. Important *and* urgent? You'd better believe it.

Mary Redding is your training supervisor. It was Mary who put this program together for your approval, and it was she who hired the speaker. Right now, she's in one of the conference rooms putting together next year's conference schedule with her instructional staff. She left word with her secretary that she was not to be disturbed. You disturb her, of course; her project is important, but it isn't urgent. This one is. Does Mary resent the interruption of what she considers a high-priority project? In this case, certainly not. But let's look at another case in which she might react differently.

The setting is the same as before. The call you receive is from the vice-president of sales. His travel schedule is such that he won't be able to attend the opening session of your sales meeting, but he will be back in time for the closing day. Could he speak to the group as a windup rather than as a keynoter? You, of course, say that will be fine. What that means, however, is that you do the kickoff in his place. Other than that, there's no problem.

You call Mary's office. She should know about this change in plan. Her secretary tells you that Mary is tied up in a meeting, but that she can take a message to her. It's 11 o'clock. You tell Mary's secretary that you'd like Mary to see you before she goes to lunch. Good going. The matter was important but not so urgent that it had to push another important matter off the boards. The urgency is on your back, however, and you set about to redo the talk you intended to give. By the time Mary walks into your office, you have the matter well in hand.

Another situation . . . same setting. In looking over the file on the upcoming meeting, you discover that Mary has approved menus for each meal. Ordinarily you wouldn't bother reviewing such minor details, but the menu for the Thursday evening dinner catches your eye. Asparagus. Mr. Hopkins, your president, indicated that he *might* be able to come to that dinner, and you recall a time that you were with Mr. Hopkins and he didn't eat his asparagus. You make a note of it. You might tell Mary to call the hotel and get a different vegetable served. It's neither urgent nor important. Later today you can discuss it.

You say that the foregoing illustrations are simple and obvious. Simple, to be sure, but most managers can point to similar situations that were handled so very differently. The *urgent* versus *important* judgment is one that is not only a daily occurrence but often an hourly one. The flat truth is that many managers don't make good judgments in this regard. Wherever you find a manager who is indiscriminate in designating importance and urgency, you'll find a manager who is chasing his or her tail and running in circles. You'll also find a manager who is driving subordinates out of their skulls. That's where middle managers find their jobs more annoying than satisfying.

Moreover, managers who attach urgency and importance to things that are neither urgent nor important often end up with egg on their faces. They lose respect and credibility with their subordinates. Just for fun, let's take the case of you, Mr. Hopkins, and the asparagus. We'll show how to make the trivial tremendous—urgent handling of the unimportant. Instant replay. . . .

You spot the asparagus on the menu, and you remember that time when Hopkins didn't eat his asparagus. Unhesitatingly, you stalk into the conference room, upset Mary's meeting, and ask Mary to step into the hall. She comes out with a concerned look on her face.

"I didn't want to break up your meeting, Mary, but I was going over the file on the sales meeting and noticed that you have ordered asparagus for the dinner on Thursday."

Mary, who hadn't paid attention to anything except the meat and potatoes, says, "Oh, I can change that if you'd like. What would you prefer?"

"Well, I really don't care, as long as it isn't asparagus. You see, Mr. Hopkins may attend, and I was with him one time when he pushed his asparagus aside, so we don't want to offend him."

"I'll call the hotel. Broccoli, brussels sprouts, fresh beans . . . take your pick."

"Broccoli . . . that'll be fine. Have them put some hollandaise sauce on it."

Mary goes back into the conference room. Her staff asks, "What was that all about?" She replies, "We made a change in the dinner menu for the sales meeting." She might have said, "Asparagus."

Sequel: Thursday night arrives. So does Mr. Hopkins. So does the broccoli. Hopkins pushes it aside. It turns out that he doesn't care for *any* vegetables except those served in a salad.

Picture another scenario. You are a manager of a very busy department. You are shorthanded. The timetable on your projects is tight. You take work home at night and on weekends. You are one of five members on a senior manager's staff. Each of you feels that you have a legitimate claim for equal time on your boss's calendar, but you discover that some people are more equal than others. Three of the managers are old buddies of the boss, and he makes time for them whenever they want it. You and the remaining manager share the discomfort of cooling your heels in the outer office or of making an "appointment" of sorts—"Will you tell Fred that I'd like to see him when he has a few minutes to talk. Call me, please."

Your fellow manager and you commiserate with each other. "He never responds to my calls faster than in about five hours," says your friend. "I don't think he wants to talk about what *I* want to talk about. In his opinion, my department is one of those operations that runs by itself and doesn't need prompt attention."

You reply: "I don't think he wants my department under his control. He has no understanding of what we really do. He told me one time that it was a compliment to me that he didn't poke around in my affairs—that I should just keep up the good work. That's O.K., but there are times when his decision has to come to bear on things. I feel obliged to report, but he doesn't feel obliged to respond."

The two of you conclude that Fred files reports from both your departments under "miscellaneous." You also conclude that he files his call slips in the round file at the corner of his desk. You further agree that the only thing more annoying than his ignoring you is his inviting you up "to talk things over," an experience that usually goes something like this:

You walk into Fred's office and are greeted like a long-lost buddy. "How the hell are you? Gosh, it's been a while. I get your reports, and they look great. You're right on top of things. Now, what was it you wanted to talk about?"

"Fred, there's the matter of funding this new program we've been asked to handle. . . ."

The telephone rings. It's Fred's secretary; you can see her in the outer office. Fred picks up the phone, listens, says, "Put him on." There follows a conversation with someone—lots of joking mixed with a little serious discussion. Five minutes later, Fred is off the phone. He makes a few notes on a pad, calls his secretary in, and says, "See that Jud gets this, and have him come up to see me as soon as he's handled it."

"O.K. Sorry. You were saying. . . ."

"I was saying, Fred, that we've been directed to develop that program on the new product. As you know, I have no money in the budget for that, and. . . ."

Jud walks in. There follows a little exchange on a topic you know is neither urgent nor important, then a little chitchat on the closing prices on the big board. You're included in this, and that's nice, but the whole affair takes five minutes more. Jud leaves, and you get back to the problem you want to solve.

Fred tells you that there is no way on earth you're going to get additional budget, and you're just about to reply that you have a suggestion: You can reallocate funds from another program, but you wanted to give him some choice in which program to drop. You don't get the alternatives out of your mouth, though, because the phone rings again. Fred's secretary isn't at her desk, so Fred swings around and answers the call.

Half an hour later, you're still trying to get a decision out of Fred. You conclude that it would have been better to have written a memo or to have gone ahead and killed another program, even if it weren't approved. Anything to avoid the frustration of having the telephone and drop-in callers take precedence over the real business of the day. It's small consolation to learn from others on Fred's staff that that's the way Fred customarily operates. He isn't a particularly good time manager.

People who manage time poorly create problems not only for themselves but for everyone else. The telephone is their little table-top god; who knows, the next call might be from *the president of the company*! In Fred's case, he's had a few calls from the president, but they didn't take very long. Fred's answer was generally a quick, "Yes, sir." It's the calls from nonpresidents that waste the time of his managers, who have better things to do than listen to Fred's half of a conversation.

The example just given is true. I've been in Fred's office. Maybe you have a Fred in your company, too.

For those managers who want to save the time of their subordinate managers and supervisors and lend dignity to the work they do and the positions they occupy, here are a few thoughts on office behavior:

• Begin with a hard look at the composition of your staff. If, indeed, some functions reporting to you are unworthy of your attention, those functions should be reassigned to someone else. If you judge that all functions are important to the achievement of your department's objectives, consider them equally deserving of your time and attention.

• Recognize that your subordinates, if they are properly executing their responsibilities, have schedules and commitments that deserve keeping. People who are readily interruptible either don't have a plan or aren't keeping to that plan.

• Remember that managers and supervisors, in the main, have worked hard to achieve the status they enjoy, and to undermine that status not only is a personal blow to the individuals but also has a subtractive effect on their relationships with those below them in the organization.

• Grunt-type work—and it does occur in all organizations—should be assigned to a supervisor with the understanding that he or she will find a person to do it. Too often, a subordinate takes on work out of classification because the manager implies that it is a personal assignment.

• Separate business life from personal life and business tasks from personal tasks. And don't pretend that a request for what is really a personal favor has a business connection.

• Save yourself and others time by holding staff meetings in which you can not only make assignments but can also learn what activities are taking place at any given time.

• Require your subordinates to file weekly or monthly reports and/or forward plans on activities within their group. These need not be detailed to the point that they generate resistance to the paperwork parade. Once established, such a system tends to be both self-perpetuating and self-disciplining.

• Rigidly discipline yourself to evaluate every situation that requires special assignments to your staff members. The difference between what is important, urgent, both, or neither dictates the way the assignment should be made and the way it will be received.

• Create a workable plan to minimize interruptions throughout the department. This will not only save you time, but it will save time and reduce frustration for others. A sample of such a policy, simply stated, might be:

> Walk-in interruptions, unless considered urgent, show little consideration for those being interrupted. When visiting someone else's office, wait until invited in. Don't break into meetings in progress. When in your own office, apply the same rules to your visitors.
>
> Alert secretaries to intercept calls when people are in your office. Politely ask if you can call back or be called. Obviously, certain incoming calls will be given priority, but the priority list should be limited.

• Bunch outgoing calls. Arrange for certain private periods throughout the day. When your staff begins to recognize that there is some routine or plan to *your* day, they'll begin to build *their* day accordingly.

• Maintain an open-door policy but learn to close the door at times.

• Do unto others as you would have them do unto you.

There are those who will say that these recommendations are commendable but unworkable. If you say so, they are. Never try it, and it will never succeed. I hasten to add that it may be beyond the control of middle management people to effect changes upward, but it is well within their province to control what lies below. Yet I have seen it work both ways: Examples set below sometimes do catch on above.

There are organizations, and then there are *other* organizations. In the same company, you will find noise, confusion, rudeness, and

thoughtlessness in one sector and the total absence of these conditions in another. It isn't just a matter of formality versus informal-
ity, either. After working for several corporations and, more recently, being a visitor in many others, my conclusions are that the
greater the quiet observance of courtesy and protocol, the greater
the mutual respect and the ultimate productivity.

When the manager makes it a point to respect the importance of
others—in terms of time, attention, and appropriate assignment of
duties—the following benefits accrue to the lower-level manager:

○ A sense that the job held, the title given, and the relationship
  enjoyed are ones of dignity and worth. Notwithstanding some
  rightfully aimed comments that some of the middle managers'
  problems stem from their own erroneous evaluation of their
  position and prerogatives, self-esteem is vital to effective management performance. Milton said it well in *Paradise Lost:*
  "Oft times nothing profits more than self-esteem, grounded on
  just and right *well managed."* (I italicized "well managed.")
○ A strengthened commitment to the role in which the manager
  is cast. When I believe that *you* believe that what I'm doing is
  important, I'll pay more attention to what I'm doing and how
  I'm doing it.
○ Freedom to apply similar treatment below. The trickle-down
  effect has to begin somewhere.

And to the manager come these benefits:

○ A team to manage—a whole that is greater than the sum of its
  parts.
○ A return of respect for respect.
○ Fewer corner-bar conversations about how the old man
  doesn't function in the staff's best interests.
○ Less infighting.
○ A growing recognition upstairs that if the department is run-
  ning well, there must be a good manager heading it.

Build a reputation for according respect and seeing things in proper perspective. When the day comes that you *have* to say, "I know you folks are busy, but this is really important," you'll get volunteers instead of having to pick draftees.

11

Shoulder to Shoulder . . .
Until the Going Gets Tough

The boss approved your forward plan but wouldn't defend it upstairs. The issue was controversial, so she stayed out of it. When your project bombed out, your name was freely mentioned in the report; when it succeeded, only the boss's name was on it. Your budget request met no resistance, because it was carved up by your boss before it was forwarded. The program you had counted on to meet your objectives got wiped out, because he found it more convenient to apply the cutback across the board rather than selectively.

Maybe you recall the old joke about the father who stood at the bottom of the steps and urged his youngster to jump. "Daddy will catch you," he said. The child hesitated, and the father repeated the pledge. So the kid jumped, and his old man stepped out of the way. As the child picked himself up, the father said, "Let that be a lesson to you: Don't trust anybody!"

The humor is faulty, but the analogy is clear. This sort of thing occurs so frequently in business situations that many middle managers develop a distrusting and cynical view of their bosses. They feel that support from above is lacking. And it's not that they are naive enough to expect that every proposal they make will be approved and supported, but when they are given initial encouragement to move out on a particular project, they hardly expect to have the rug pulled out from under them on the slightest resistance from topside. Yet it happens often enough to stifle creativity and reasonable risk taking. And when that trickles down through an organization, losses are inevitable.

A middle management acquaintance of mine tells a typical story: He was a section manager who reported to a department manager who reported to a vice-president. Reporting to him were supervisors and specialists. He was very much in the middle. He was also a person of conviction and dedication, and he was creative—at times ahead of the technology available to him. "If only we could . . ." was a common opening statement, but he was always careful not to make a serious recommendation that was beyond implementation.

His boss, not nearly so creative nor as well informed about new technologies, nonetheless listened to most of his subordinates' suggestions. The ideas that required little expense to implement and posed little risk were generally given prompt approval. In that respect, the department manager was a pleasant and supportive executive. But when the proposal was beyond his immediate understanding, he chose to resist rather than to admit his lack of knowledge. And if the proposal had unusual expense or risk connected with it, it was tabled for "later consideration."

One day, the section manager had what he and his subordinates felt was a perfect answer to a nagging problem within the department. In fact, it had implications that would generate potentially great benefits for the corporation. It was a little far-out, compared to the traditional ways of doing things, and it involved some of the newer and more recently developed electronic equipment. Knowing the department manager's reputation for laying aside ideas not readily or easily put into the mill, the section manager and one of his supervisors labored over a presentation that clearly spelled out the plan and the personnel and capital requirements. They also meticulously listed the benefits and put the proposal into a form that could be used by the department manager to sell the idea to the vice-president.

Armed with three neatly bound copies of the proposal, Bob, the section manager, and Adam, one of his supervisors, made their way to the office of Jim, the department manager. They had even taken care to make a specific appointment—not a customary arrangement in most cases.

"Jim," said Bob, "we made this a special occasion, because we have what we believe to be a special proposal. It's the solution to a problem we've talked about often, but for which we hadn't come up with good answers. Now we believe we have them."

There followed a careful, comprehensive presentation of the idea. Jim was impressed with the work that had gone into it. He even acknowledged that it was worth processing upward. "I'll run it by J.B. and the other department managers at our next staff meeting. Yes, I think it deserves looking into. Nice work, fellows."

A few days later, Bob inquired about the project. "Oh," said Jim, "I brought it up at our last staff meeting, and the general consensus was that it was too costly to handle right now. We can put it into next year's forward plan and budget request. Hang onto the proposal; we'll get back to it later."

A month went by. One day, Bob got so tied up that it was nearly 1:30 P.M. before he could break for lunch. The management dining room was closed, so he walked across the street to a little diner. Harvey, another department manager, was sitting there and waved him over. While they ate, Harvey made a fleeting reference to the problem at which Bob's proposal had been aimed. Bob said, "Yeah, it's too bad Jim got shot down on that. We thought we had a good solution."

"Jim got shot down on what? What solution did you propose?"

Bob knew he was trapped but went ahead and explained the essence of the proposal. Harvey thought that was a great idea; it was evident this was the first he had heard about it. Bob could read what had happened in the staff meeting, but he was too polite to pursue it. The truth was that Jim, intimidated by talk about tight money and careful budget administration, had never brought the proposal up. The support on which Bob had counted just wasn't there. His boss was one of those weathervane managers, who never sail into even the lightest breeze.

Another case: Everett, a valued supervisor, had made a tactical error that resulted in damage to a piece of equipment vital to day-to-day operations. The repair of that equipment was not only costly but caused a delay that came to the attention of top management. The furor broke in the office of Everett's manager, who not only was aware of the problem but had inadvertently given Everett tacit approval to misuse the equipment. It had been one of those cases of, "I'm too busy to discuss that now, so use your own judgment."

When the vice-president stormed into the manager's office and launched a tirade, Everett's boss did the classic cop-out. "I'll see to it that it doesn't happen again, Mr. Wellborn. You can be sure of that. You'd think a supervisor with Everett's experience would know better than to be so careless. He has had a lot of instruction and counsel on things like this, but people get headstrong at times. I'll write him a letter of reprimand, and you'll get a copy of it."

Everett may or may not have heard about the vice-president's visit to his manager's office. He may or may not get a copy of the letter of reprimand, even though a copy will fly to the executive suite. He is the victim of a nonsupportive manager. It happens too often to overlook the consequences. One of these days, Everett will discover what happened, and he will have real justification for singing the middle management blues.

In an earlier chapter, we discussed the business of performance appraisals. The normal route to take on this is to have the appraisal written and discussed with subordinates, then passed on up to the superior for approval and signature, followed by transmission to the personnel department for permanent filing. One manager discovered that his boss would approve the numbers in his presence, then adjust them downward (or upward, as the case might be) before sending them on. In that way, the top manager avoided a confrontation with his subordinates yet had his own way on the ratings. Another situation in which nonsupport was displayed.

I recall a very different type of incident early in my career under one of the best managers I have ever worked for. I had been interviewing candidates for a position in my department and had attracted an unusual number of applications. Unknown to me, one of the candidates was a personal friend of an executive vice-president in the corporation. We had reviewed the applicant's credentials in a prescreening process, determined that he was poorly suited for the position, and had decided not to offer him an interview, but one morning he appeared at my office door. Since I had some time, I interviewed him.

I proceeded to point out to him as courteously as I could that his preparation and the demands of the job didn't match. I suggested that he try other departments and other companies. He was persistent, did a little name-dropping that I didn't accept gracefully but didn't think was important. (That was a mistake, but I didn't learn about it until later.) At any rate, after taking more time than the applicant deserved, I closed the interview with, "I think, Mr. Klutz, it is unlikely that we would have a place for you on this staff. If you'd like, I'll hold onto your résumé, but I don't think it will do much good. I have interviewed a number of excellent candidates and have many more to see. My decision will be made in the next two weeks. If I want to reinterview you, I'll call. Otherwise, don't expect to hear from us." Now, if *you* were told that, wouldn't you think it was final?

This fellow obviously didn't. He might not have, even if I had thrown him out of the office bodily. But he had a trump card to play. He would cause trouble for me through the office of the executive vice-president. And he did.

It happened three weeks later. I had filled the position and was pleased with my new hire. I was in my boss's office discussing a totally unrelated matter, when his telephone rang. I could hear his secretary in the outer office intercept the call, then transfer it in. The name of the executive vice-president was mentioned. My boss took the call. He listened intently . . . for a long time. I could read distress on his face. And all the while he was listening and answering, he was looking directly at me. It never occurred to me that I was the subject of the conversation, however.

He concluded the conversation with, "I'm very sorry that matter had to come to your attention, but I'll look into it and call you back within the next five minutes." When the phone had been hung up, my boss turned to me and asked if I remembered interviewing a Mr. Klutz. "Oh, sure," I said. "He was one of some nine or ten I talked to. A poor candidate. . . ."

"Well, that was Mr. Van. It seems that you interviewed a guy who has a direct line to the top floor. Van has a letter on his desk accusing you of being rude and not fulfilling a commitment to the candidate. Said you promised to write him a letter one way or the other."

I explained the incident. My boss and I agreed that what had been done was appropriate. He turned around, dialed the executive vice-president's number. "Mr. Van, I've looked into the matter of the applicant. I have the manager in my office right now. He told me that this particular candidate would not even have been invited in for an interview but showed up of his own accord without an appointment. When he was interviewed, he was told that his qualifications and the job requirements didn't match. He was given no encouragement—was actually advised at the time that he should look elsewhere. He was also told not to expect to hear from us. I'm sorry that it involved a personal friend of yours. . . ."

There followed a long period of listening.

"I'm glad you understand the situation, Mr. Van. Would it be helpful to you if we wrote the young man?"

Another long period of listening.

After hanging up, my boss turned to me and said, "Van is a real guy. He told me the kid you interviewed was a relative of someone who used to work for him. He'll write him and put the matter at rest. You're in the clear."

I thanked him for his support. He said, "I respect your judgment and thought it unlikely that you would have handled the case as badly as it was described to me. I'll always support what is supportable."

What was particularly interesting about the case just described is that there were later beneficial consequences. The executive vice-president liked the way the situation had been handled. My own opinion was that he enjoyed the way someone stood up to him. People smart enough to get to his level can see through the fawning that often surrounds them. He also liked the fact that the response was quick and certain. The department grew in his favor and attention; we were called upon to do a number of special projects, and he approved overbudget requests on at least two occasions. Support had earned support in a most interesting way.

Most of us who have wrestled with middle management roles have seen incidents that were worthy of support and others that were not. The key phrase should be: "Support what is supportable." In a very real way, that's an implied contract made when the issue is agreed upon at the manager-manager level. The managers should understand one another regarding the support to be expected. If I am your subordinate manager or supervisor, and I come to you with a proposal that lies beyond your immediate level of authority, I should expect that you will have to consult a higher authority before giving approval. My clue to the extent of your support should be in the manner in which you pledge it:

o "I'm not sure we can get this project approved, but I'll discuss it with Mac." That means you'll give it a try.
o "I really like this proposal. It has merit, and Mac should know about it. I'll try to convince him that we should find the money to put it into effect." That means you'll try harder.
o "I don't think it will fly, but I'll bring it up the next time I see Mac." That means I shouldn't expect much support from you.

Suppose that the authority to approve an action is within your scope, and I convince you that we should take that action. You may be reluctant, and you say, "I doubt that it will work, but it won't hurt to give it a try. Keep me informed on the progress, and if it doesn't look good, stop it immediately." That means you will take the responsibility as long as I work within your instructions.

"Good idea. Let's try it." That means you have given me a go-ahead and will accept all responsibility. In either case, the manager who gives approval—limited or full—pledges support and owes it to the subordinate. The subordinate should move ahead with the assurance that as long as he or she stays within the levels of authority, the boss's support goes with the approval. It can be no other way. Subordinates should expect no more, but their managers should expect to do no less.

Support from above shows itself in other ways, too. It sometimes shows on the outside. Not long ago, I took on a special assignment with a major corporation. I was impressed with the middle managers I dealt with throughout the experience. They were bright, knowledgeable, and self-assured. They had been given a responsibility to carry off a sensitive and important project, had called in an agency known for its ability to produce careful and convincing explanations, and I was a part of the agency team. Everyone rolled up sleeves and went to work with enthusiasm and assurance.

I thought I had stumbled onto a perfectly wonderful example of delegated responsibility and top management support. The middle managers had no question in their minds regarding the fact that, in each of their special areas, they had the responsibility to direct the activity and the authority to approve it. On one occasion I ventured to inquire whether the executive in charge of the project was to meet with us and give us additional input. "Oh, no," I was told. "He doesn't want to see anything until it's completed. He has said that if *we* like it, *he'll* support it."

It didn't work that way. We pulled together a remarkable piece of material. The agency brass was delighted with it. The middle managers made a few minor changes in format and technical information but thought we had a great finished product. It didn't fly. The big man came aboard and upset the apple cart. This shouldn't have been done, and who said it should, and so on. Totally new policies were set—sometimes complete reversals. Managers who had worked on the project felt let down. The rug had been snapped from under them.

Upper-level managers have the right to criticize. But they should also face up to their obligation to fulfill the implied contract of support. It's that clear and that simple. That it doesn't happen as often or as completely as it should is an ongoing complaint of many middle managers.

Managers at every level would do themselves and their subordinates a real favor if they would:

o Spell out the way the implied contract of support is to be understood by both parties.
o Encourage subordinates to operate that way, in turn, with their subordinates.
o Live up to the bargain.

When managers at all levels clearly understand their roles and the importance of living up to the implied contract, they do these things for their subordinates:

o Give them confidence to move ahead with important work, knowing that support is assured.
o Give them a sense of responsibility for doing the work as effectively and efficiently as possible.
o Make them feel a part of a team—sharing in obligations and responsibility and deserving of support for what they do.

Supportive managers do not lack their own rewards for standing up for their subordinates. Such managers get:

o Deserved respect for courage and integrity.
o Support from below.
o Improved productivity.
o The kind of constructive input that is the hallmark of the progressive organization.

One wonders why support from above isn't fully automatic and totally reliable. Much of it must stem from thoughtlessness. Some of it can probably be chalked up to indifference. A bit of it has to do with lack of courage and/or conviction. Maybe all of these shortcomings are present in some managers. Maybe that's why we like to work under the supervision of thoughtful, interested, courageous, and dedicated managers. They're the kind of managers who either give support or face up to telling their subordinates candidly why support shouldn't be expected. They can—and should—be found at every level in a good business organization.

12

Of Course We Have a Training Department, But I Don't Think It's in This Building . . .

Some parents have difficulty understanding children; they believe kids should be miniature adults, and when youthful behavior doesn't match their expectations, they contend that things aren't what they used to be. Ditto for many managers.

Performance essentially depends on two key factors: capability and attitude. The *can-do/will-do* equation, however, is ignored by managers who perceive the jobs they supervise as not too difficult. After all, that same job was once held by the manager on his or her way up. What the boss may not accept is that the job has become more complicated, it was not done particularly well when the manager did it, or the incumbent is not so naturally talented as his or her predecessor. Let's examine each of those reasons in turn.

The job has become more complicated. Consider that the efforts toward job simplification have largely been aimed at shop-type operations. What used to be grunt work has now become power-assisted. Operations that used to be skill-dependent have become machine-dependent. A case in point is right in the office: Your secretary seldom fusses with typing that requires carbon paper, because she can type an original and cover any mistakes with correcting fluid or hit the correction key on her typewriter and run the original through a copy machine. It can be filled with errors, but technology has helped bring it off right.

Management jobs have not been the beneficiaries of improved technology, however. What technology has done is make data more precise and more abundant, communications more profuse and instantaneous, and expectations greater in terms of both precision and time. Yesterday's job may be a poor measurement of today's job, and judging today's manager by what you did on that same job a few years ago may be both foolish and unfair. Let's consider one typical case of how changes may have crept in.

A field sales office is headed by a manager. He has a small staff to handle office matters and certain specialties—service, distribution, training, and promotions. He has 15 sales representatives reporting to him through an assistant manager. He, in turn, reports upward to a regional manager who reports to the vice-president of sales. Each of the upper-level managers has, at one time or another, occupied a field sales management post—the VP, ten years ago, and the regional manager, five years ago.

In ten years, the product line has almost doubled. Territories that didn't exist now flourish and account for significant volume. Competition unknown a few years back is now well established. Volume has grown, but share of market stays about the same. Five years ago, all sales reports were typed and mailed, with preliminary figures telephoned in each week. Today, all field offices are equipped with computer terminals that connect to the corporate marketing computer, and sales figures are transmitted daily. The home office has the big picture as fast as the field office has a reading on its own little corner of the world.

New demands have been placed on the field sales office manager. His job requires him to spend more time at special meetings with customers; representing the company at civic affairs and at state legislatures, where new rules, regulations, and prohibitions affect his industry; and at regional staff meetings, where new programs are constantly being introduced. Market research people from the home office fly in on a moment's notice and involve him in their studies. Few, if any, of these things were done five years ago; practically none ten years ago. Yet the manager's bosses believe that the job is much the same today as it was when they occupied it—perhaps even a little simpler.

The job *is* perhaps more interesting and less paper-cluttered. Less routine and office-centered, to be sure. But simpler? Certainly not. Even more important, the training that made the manager of five or ten years ago a functional and productive individual is far from the type of training needed in the present situation. Some managers fail to recognize this or refuse to admit it if they do. Is it a blind spot, or is it a case of "What was good enough for me is good enough for them."?

The job was not done particularly well when the former manager occupied it. This cuts a little close to the bone, but most of us have known cases of this sort. It's a little like the hue and cry made over the years about why Johnnie can't read. The trouble is that the complaints are often made by parents who weren't so adept at it either. Yet to hear them discuss school systems, you'd think they attended the very best and learned the very most. Show me. And show me the records of some managers who shake their heads over the performances of their subordinates and say, "When I was. . . ." A little soul-searching is in order.

We have come through an extended period of growth in industry. Thousands of managers have been force-fed through the hungry system. Some had scarcely warmed the chairs to which they were assigned, when the calls came for them to move on. These managers represent various levels of competence. Some are high-potential people destined for top management, and others are examples of the Peter Principle: Given the opportunity, they will rise to their own level of incompetence. Managers at either end of the pole don't always have all the seasoning or exposure necessary to make the claim that they truly held a position and functioned well in it.

A good example of the move-'em-through promotion school are some women managers. I have heard of many cases in which women were rushed through the chairs in order to support the claim that equal rights were a reality in a given company. Granted, some succeed, and it must be added that it is not only right but sensible that women be given the opportunity to fill management roles. But unfortunately, the woman who doesn't measure up to standards in her management job is criticized because she is a *woman,* not because she is the victim of an accelerated promotion program. Male or female, if managers move *through* jobs rather than *to* and *from* them, they are not likely to understand the full impact of those jobs. And the chances are good that while they filled the spot, their eyes were focused elsewhere. Should we be surprised when they don't perform the job fully or well?

The incumbent doesn't have the talent his or her boss had. I have often claimed that people in middle management do a sour-grapes routine when they say of top management, "They lucked in, had pull, were on the right corner at the right time. They're no more talented than you or I." Sure, all of us know of cases where there are people down in the middle ranks who are smarter than those on the top floor. But take a good look at those who rise to the top. They have talent, or they wouldn't stay up there very long.

I know some people who now lead companies but weren't particularly great performers when they were on their way up. For instance, I worked with a man who was fairly ordinary in his performance at the bottom and in the middle, but circumstances put him in a very good position, from which he rose quickly. And, what do you know—he was pretty good upstairs! Talent often has to find its own time and place.

As managers rise in the corporate ladder, they often look down on subordinates as being less talented than they. That's fine if they make an effort to develop subordinates' skills in such a way as to offset the lack. But in many cases, they don't. They leave it where it is and continue to complain about it. They follow a self-serving logic pattern that goes like this:

- I shouldn't have hired Roger in the first place.
- If it weren't for the fact that nobody else was available, we shouldn't have promoted him to his present job.

o He has too much service to fire him; besides, there's nobody
   else who's a lot better.
o Maybe, in time, Roger will improve.
o Being the boss isn't a bed of roses!

Overlooked in all this is the need for training. By that, I mean
specific training for the job in which an individual is now placed as
well as training for the job he or she is slated to take. I also mean
continuing training, which may be broadening to the individual
rather than specific to the job. It is every manager's responsibility
to evaluate the training needs of individuals in the department and
to provide opportunity to satisfy those needs. This is not something
that is done by the personnel department or the training department; it is done in the manager's own office, with his or her head
buried in the records, not in the sand. The training process begins
with the manager for whom the training is done.

In some ways, the best training is that done by the manager. Yet
managers have many ways of skirting the problem. That is especially true with respect to their immediate subordinates. A plant
manager will see to it that people in the shop are trained, but the
staff members can shift for themselves. A sales manager may insist
that sales representatives under his or her supervision get rigorous
training, but the manager's own assistant can't be released for a
seminar. It is probably the result of the manager's belief that he or
she didn't have training on the way up, and "If I made it, so can
they." What folly it is to perpetuate a wrong!

As a former training manager, I may be overly sensitive to this
condition. Ours was a very large operation in a very large company. We trained as many as 15,000 people a year—both our own
corporate sales personnel and dealer personnel who sold our product. There were times when we literally forced our services on
people, because we saw the need for help. There were other times
when we were invited in to do seminars or workshops on certain
topics for individual departments. Over many years, I made a number of observations regarding the difference between sessions ini-

tiated by the training organization and those initiated by the manager.

When the training department called the meetings:

- o The department manager generally had to go to New York, Chicago, San Francisco, or at least to someone else's office.
- o The higher-graded staff members slipped in and out of the conference room, presumably to take or make important phone calls.
- o Overall group participation was good, and conference comment sheets filled out at the close of the meeting simply indicated appreciation for what had been done.

When the department management called the meetings:

- o The department manager kicked off the session and showed support for the program.
- o Activity was full and constant, and in those cases where a participant had to be called out, that person always made it a point to apologize later to the instructor.
- o Participation was lively, and at times, the group waived or shortened coffee breaks and luncheon periods. Postconference comments were specific—in fact, they were sometimes critical of our not having covered in sufficient depth a subject the participant wanted more help on.

A further observation: In most situations, the department whose management initiated training and kept some sort of development activity going at all times was the department that performed well, had high morale, and bred good managers for other departments!

Organizations are interesting. They tend to take on the attitudinal profile of their leaders. Within a single company, there can be many different attitudes, and those attitudes can almost always be traced upward. Whether this stems from a desire to curry favor above, or whether it is an unconsciously learned behavior is a moot question. My suspicion is that it is some of both. I feel safe in making certain comparisons as this relates to training, because my exposure in that field has been considerable. My recollections of General Electric are of a company not only amenable to training but supportive of it. My recollections of Chrysler are of pockets of enthusiasm and pockets of indifference. And although the automotive industry as a whole spends enormous amounts of money on training, it doesn't seem to attach the importance to it that I've noticed in working with pharmaceuticals companies. Those are observations, not conclusions.

Every company I've ever known has its high and low spots. One product goes over big, another doesn't. One plant operates at a high quality level, another doesn't. One sales region hums along well, while another bumps along the bottom. There are a lot of contributing factors, to be sure, but training deserves to be looked at as a possibility. But sometimes, unfortunately, it isn't even considered at all.

I was a close observer of a sales organization that had many regional offices. Among those offices, two or three at any one time were trouble spots. They could readily be identified, because they routinely fell below the corporate average in share of market and profitability. They received significant attention from upper-level managers. They were frequently visited, became the object of intensified advertising and sales promotion campaigns, and were the scenes of management rotation. They were seldom much fun to hold training sessions in, because marginal conference attendance was predictable. "We have so many *important* things to do . . ." "If you could come back in three months . . ." "You just don't understand this market . . . It's different."

Conversely, there were regions where quotas were always met, where managers seemed to get everything done on time, where training activities were a way of life. Subordinate managers from those regions made excellent candidates for promotion to higher posts in other regions. But (one of the ironies of life) these were seldom the people who were sent to the troubled regions. One time I heard that it was because they weren't considered capable of managing in a crisis. Of course not: They were the people who kept crises from happening! They were also the people who, when assigned to a management post, worked smoothly and constructively with their subordinates. Like begets like, and patterns are set that way.

In the training business, there is a process called the training needs analysis. It is usually conducted by the training department or by an outside consulting organization that is especially qualified to come up with usable information. Done properly, the needs analysis consults at least two parties: the individual for whom training is intended and the supervisor for whom that individual works. "What do *you* think you need to know or be able to do that you don't presently know or aren't capable of doing" is matched with, "What do you think *your subordinate* needs to know . . . ?" It is presumed that the melding of responses will lead to the establishment of an appropriate line of action.

Whenever one of these surveys is conducted, you find a number of interesting things:

o Managers who are closer to their subordinates and more interested in their development come up with better answers than those who are not so close or interested.

o Subordinates of the former type of manager provide answers that are close to their boss's; subordinates of the latter type of manager don't.

o Needs lists of managers who are training-oriented aim less at fundamentals and more at refinements. Fundamentals have already been taken care of with on-the-job training.

o Interested and supportive managers are eager to know the results of the analysis and to get whatever training is indicated off and running.

We did a triple-header one time with several hundred automobile dealerships. We surveyed dealers with respect to their assessment of the training needs of their sales managers and sales representatives. At the same time, we asked the sales managers what training was needed by sales representatives, and that was followed by a survey of the salespeople themselves. The better, more circumspect answers came from the successful dealers and the productive sales managers. They not only knew what their subordinates needed to know, but they also knew what they themselves didn't know. They knew where they could help themselves, and they knew where they would like to have outside help. The answers that came from salespeople weren't, "I'd like to learn how to close a deal." They said, "I'd like to be able to close deals more easily for both the prospect and myself."

Those were business organizations where volume was achieved and profits were made. Their turnover was lower than in many other operations of like size and location. They also enjoyed the best customer relations. They needed less training than people in many other dealerships, but they wanted it more. What is particularly germane to this discussion on middle management is the fact that the sales managers in these dealerships seemed to demonstrate a very high degree of proprietary interest, dealer loyalty, and concern for subordinates.

Training is not something you do only when things aren't going well. Of course you do it then, if that's what's necessary. The real reason for training is to forestall difficulties and emergencies. You do it so that you can rid yourself of half of what is often mistakenly regarded as a motivational problem. If you've attended to the *can-do* part of the performance equation, the *will-do* part becomes more easily identifiable and correctable. The odds are in favor of the *can-do* erasing a fair amount of the *will-do* problem.

There are a number of enrichment areas all middle managers will profit from, assuming that they first understand their jobs and possess the basic skills that allow them to function in them. Development of these enrichment skills may not only improve performance on the present job but provide a base from which an individual can reach out for greater responsibility and recognition. Opportunity, after all, is one of the things middle management people seek, and recognition is another. We do subordinates a favor by encouraging self-development, and that favor is returned to us many times over, in improved attitudes and performance.

Some of the more likely enrichment areas that are helpful to middle managers are motivation, problem solving, decision making, communications skills, goal setting, managerial psychology, management styles. It makes little difference whether one is a manager in manufacturing, marketing, finance, engineering, personnel, or any other discipline; these enhancement skills can be applied to the managerial job. Programs of these types are readily available in a variety of formats. Universities offer them in their business extension services. Organizations like the American Management Associations have a busy schedule throughout the year and make the courses available at locations across the country. Consultants and agencies offer selected programs. Many programs are available in home-study packages. And what about your own training department? You may have an expert on some of these subjects on staff. If the training office isn't in this building, it may be right next door.

Another range of training needs to consider is skill updating. Your managers might be current in their specialties, but chances are they aren't. Consider the engineer who left the university five or ten years ago. If he or she hasn't been sent back to explore the new technology, you're missing something very important. Office procedures have changed dramatically in recent years, with the introduction of more data processing and data communications. What can be embarrassing is the case in which a new employee enters the organization and is more in touch with the latest developments than the boss. If managers are to lead, they had better be ahead themselves.

Reconsider the training needs of subordinates on a regular basis. It's an area that should be explored during every performance review. It should also be considered whenever a job description is rewritten. Even without conducting a careful professional analysis, training needs can easily be discovered if you ask yourself just a few basic questions:

- What's happening that I don't want to happen?
- What's not happening that I do want to happen?
- What has changed in recent times that calls for new knowledge and new skills?
- What will be needed in the individual's next assignment that isn't evident now?
- Is there anyone here who could step into my place if I moved up tomorrow?
- Will taking care of the above-listed training needs improve my own chances of moving up? (The answer to the last point generally is yes.)

Care has to be exercised in providing training to management-level people. The communication process is important; we can't leave people with the impression that they have been selected for training because they're incapable. That's what often happens, and it makes the medicine so bitter that the cure may seem not worth its taking. Training, properly presented, offers an opportunity for improved performance—greater self-assurance, higher achievement, better odds for self-fulfillment.

And another caution: Training should never be presented as a ticket to promotion. That mistake is often made, later to be regretted by both superior and subordinate. General Motors appears to have a genius for developing more candidates than there are positions available. But its people seem to understand that. In filling upper-level positions, the question isn't, "Where will I look for a candidate?" It's simply, "Which one will I choose?"

Training-conscious managers do a number of beneficial things for the organization and the people in it. They

- Help people acquire skills equal to the task.
- Put middle managers in a position to work independently and interactingly.
- Give subordinates a sense of assurance.
- Fit subordinates to identify problems and solve them rather than wait for tasks to be assigned.

○ Set a pattern for middle managers, in turn, to encourage further development downward.
○ Prepare subordinates for the unusual and the unexpected.
○ Give them a deserved sense of individual accomplishment.
○ Make goals reasonable by helping managers acquire the skills to attain them.
○ Prepare people for opportunities on both an individual and a group basis.

And by doing all this, managers do a few very nice things for themselves. They

○ Eliminate the limitations on delegation by making sure that the job can be done.
○ Free up time for planning and creativity—time that might otherwise be taken up supervising and correcting performance.
○ Get more done.
○ Receive recognition from upstairs as being managers who know how to get things done efficiently and effectively.

There are some managers who live their whole lives playing the scavenger. They survive because they beg, borrow, or steal capable people from someone else. We know that. But we also know that the time will come when the scavenger is given the golden opportunity to go in new directions. Faced with that kind of situation, the training-minded manager simply starts by developing people to support his or her program. The nontrainer fails. Opting to be a trainer is an easy choice to make.

When you see your present organization as your very own company and your success as dependent on your development of people to implement *your* objectives, you begin to train people or you find out quickly where the training department is located!

13

I Meant to Tell You, Lieutenant . . .
Have the Troops Explain the Battle Plan

Business communication has matured considerably in the last three decades. Some of it has to do with the proliferation of media, some with the growing curiosity of the population. We have become accustomed to getting news about so many things, why not get inside information about our business? A lot of it is the result of the insistence of organized labor that it has a right to the facts affecting its deliberation and negotiation with management; how can it play against a stacked deck? Another part of the maturity can be traced to management's recognition that informed workers are better producers—assuming, of course, that the information workers have is both understandable and believable. And acceptable from their point of view—add that.

If your age allows you to remember back as far as mine does, you may recall an era when "tell 'em nothing" was standard operating procedure. Then there were the house organs, with their cheerleading messages—sugar-coated stories about the product's popularity but never a hint about its profitability. And what about the employee meetings we used to have? Often they came around Christmas, and we got the traditional ham or turkey. Then management's holiday greetings, which seemed always to end with, "And if we all work hard next year. . . ."

We've outgrown that. Sure, it still exists in hundreds of companies, but it no longer constitutes the norm for what we would call "employee communications." The validity of house organs and employee meetings has improved with management's increased willingness to share real information with people involved in the enterprise. We have come to recognize that straight information in the hands of responsible people can work to our benefit.

We used to classify information and audiences this way:

○ Must be communicated—to everyone.
○ Could be communicated—to certain levels.
○ Should be withheld—from most levels.
○ Must be withheld—from everyone.

That's faintly reminiscent of the reasoning that surrounded Watergate. That unfortunate event triggered a common demand that what you are privileged to know, I'm privileged to know too. The underlying philosophy is that information which will affect my personal life and well-being is my right to have. But that idea can fall through the cracks in many ways, so management properly maintains the right to release some kinds of information and withhold others. The other issue at stake is how far down in an organization does certain information go, and how does it get there? That's where middle managers often have understandable frustrations and justifiable complaints.

One middle manager explained his company's communications policy this way: "We operate like a mushroom farm. They keep us in the dark and heap all kinds of manure on us." Another put it like this: "If it's good news, the boss holds the meeting. If it's bad, I'm the official spokesman." Still a third said, "If I'm out of town and call in to one of my supervisors, and he tells me something I should have had the responsibility of telling *him*, I cross it off to geography. But if I'm right there in the office, and a subordinate comes up with some newsy bit, I find that inexcusable." So do I, but it happens.

Some managements exercise infinite care to be sure that the levels of responsibility and communication are appropriately matched. I have long since forgotten the nature of the information, but I will not forget the circumstances surrounding one such exhibition of care. I was called in by my boss one afternoon at five o'clock and asked if I was in a position to drive to another plant location that evening. I said I was. "Can you be back here, packed and ready to go, by seven o'clock?" I said I could. He could read my unspoken questions. "We have a program that will affect a lot of people at all plant locations. We want the story to break simultaneously, and we want it to be told properly. You're going to take the message and the materials down to Charlie, explain it to him, and stay on for the meeting he'll hold. I'll give you the details at seven. Meanwhile, all you have to tell anyone is that you're going down to see Charlie."

I raced home, packed, bolted down some dinner, and got back to the office. My boss was packed—ready to go to a third plant in the system. We went over the program together. It was already arranged that the plant managers at each location would be available at eight o'clock the next morning. We hit the road, each of us facing a four- or five-hour drive to towns not reachable by air. I felt like the pony express riders of old . . . letter-to-García . . . cloak-and-dagger . . . 007.

At eight o'clock the next morning, I met with Charlie, the plant manager. When he had digested the details of the program, he called in his staff. He explained it to them. They arranged an employee meeting, and it was held according to plan. The program was carried off successfully.

Today, with improved communications techniques, the whole thing could have been done differently: telecommunications for the message and courier service for the materials. But the strict observance regarding the precision of the information and the flow-through of the system couldn't have been improved upon. As a very young supervisor, I was most impressed, and the concept has never left me. It has made me uncomfortable and annoyed at times, though, because I have so often seen the communications process handled poorly.

Open communication has its dangers, to be sure. In 1981, we saw a case of communications backfire when the CEO of a major corporation felt obliged to address a rumor that involved not only his business life but his personal life as well. A very modern manager, product of the Harvard School of Business, and thoroughly imbued with up-to-date ideas about communications, this CEO had hired a recent MBA to serve as his administrative assistant. They worked together, traveled together, attended civic and social affairs together—just another corporate bigwig and his assistant. The only rub was that the assistant, in addition to being a very sharp businessperson, was a young and attractive woman.

The assistant was subsequently appointed to a position of greater responsibility and power. There followed some internal strife at high levels. The CEO thought that calling an employee meeting and explaining the young lady's talents as well as disclaiming any personal relationship would quell the rumors. The inside meeting became a public affair, because certain unhappy managers quietly invited the press to attend. It became a cause célèbre and resulted in the young lady's resignation. Many observers believe that the communications fault was not just the mass meeting but the failure to handle the communications problem within the inner circle of managers.

Sometimes even the most careful communications efforts fail to get the ideas across. Mighty General Motors, much in the news and staffed with professional communicators throughout its mammoth organization, suffered record-breaking losses in 1980 and 1981. It had layoffs just as the other car companies had, and its misfortunes were widely publicized, internally and externally. Yet when it conducted a survey among its employees after several quarters of massive losses, it discovered that a majority of them thought their company was a big money maker! (Maybe the president of Chrysler wasn't totally wrong when, a number of years back, he eliminated his communications department in a companywide cutback not long after having been named "Communicator of the Year" by the chamber of commerce.)

Some communications require designated organizational control and assistance. It would be impossible for each level of management to carry on its own communications program. It is often helpful to have the president of the company appear personally before the entire body of employees. And there is nothing wrong with the manager of a department holding sessions with everyone in that department. That isn't what the middle management complaint is about. What middle managers decry is being bypassed or ignored in the communications process. They like to be in on things, if only a few minutes ahead of the crowd. They like to be credited with the intelligence and trust they believe their position deserves.

What some middle managers fail to recognize, however, is that they don't always deserve the trust they think they should have. There will always be privileged information in a business meeting. A topic discussed at a staff meeting is not, ipso facto, a topic for distribution down the line. I recall an incident in which the closing of a plant was discussed at a meeting as a remote possibility—something still in the speculative stage, and certainly not an expected event. Within an hour after the meeting broke up, the rumor was widespread. It was no longer speculation; it was a certainty. This kind of mismanagement of information often keeps upper levels of management from sharing their thoughts with managers and supervisors at the next lower level.

If we agree that it is necessary and desirable to distribute information properly throughout a business organization, we ought to take a hard look at what should be done to make the process workable. In doing so, we should lay down some guidelines that can be incorporated into the system at whatever level a manager may be. This is consistent with a point of view expressed earlier—that managers can effect good management practices downward, even though they may not be able to effect them upward. So, whether you are the president, vice-president, director, manager, or supervisor, you are in control of what passes below. Here are some suggestions:

First, make careful judgment with respect to the information.

• Is the information already labeled secret, confidential, or nobody's business? Keep it that way. If someone has taken the pains to identify certain information as unsuitable for further transmission, so be it.

• Is the information important to the proper execution of responsibilities within your own organization? Is the information vital to your organization's proper interaction with another organization? Is the information applicable to the whole organization or just to a part of it? Unless it deals solely with one or two individuals, it qualifies for staff distribution. If it applies to individuals and is of no consequence to the group, it should be reserved for individual consultation.

• Is it information you have received from reliable sources?

• Is it information you understand well enough to explain it properly? In other words, do you feel confident about passing it on to others? If not, consider asking for help.

Then, consider the format and circumstances in which you will pass the information on. This takes preparation:

Will it be an oral explanation? Make careful notes.

Would it be better written? Write it.

Is it something you feel your subordinates should pass down to still another level? Provide notes and/or copies of the written material to your subordinates.

Finally, the process itself:

• Arrange to have all persons who should receive the information available at the same time and place. This is one of the great advantages of having set staff meetings that take precedence over routine business: Affected parties are always present.

• Establish an understanding regarding your attitude about confidentiality. Make it clear that when you indicate the need for further dissemination of certain information, you want it passed along. Make it equally clear that when you identify other information as not to go beyond this level, you will not ignore leaks or the person who makes them.

• Present the information with all the clarity you can bring to bear. Invite questions and provide answers. Be sure that understanding exists, particularly when the subordinate's role is to pass the information downward.

• Encourage prompt relaying of information down if that is the action you want taken.

• If data and other materials have been prepared for distribution, be sure everyone gets them.

It is important to cultivate a sense of trust among your subordinates. When you tell them that you have no more information than you have provided them, it had better be true. If you do have additional information and are not privileged to give them more than you have, tell them that when more can be made available, you'll be the first to give it to them. Play no games and play no favorites.

And what about rumors? How should they be dealt with? Again, there are a few time-honored ground rules for that:

• Accustom your subordinates to discuss any rumors they hear with you *first*. What you will learn could be the cause of some embarrassment for you, particularly if your manager isn't a good communicator. Often the word gets around the secretarial pool before it hits the department office.

• Keep your staff from being the spreaders of rumors. The term "scuttlebutt" comes from the old navy label for the water barrel. When sailors were thirsty, they went to the barrel, and that's where they gossiped. Two supervisors discussing a rumor at the water cooler are simply a modern-day version of the old routine.

• Pursue your own manager for information. If he or she is a good communicator, you'll get it automatically. If not, ask. Your own boss may be as sensitive to rumors as anyone, so pass the rumors—and the courtesy—upward.

• Don't start rumors of your own. Distinguish speculation from fact and label speculation as such. Get the reputation for delivering straight talk.

I said earlier that any manager at any level can control the communications process downward in the organization. I didn't claim that by doing so that manager would enjoy complete immunity from poor communications. You can get the rug pulled from under you by noncommunicating superiors. I recall a case of a rumored cutback in personnel that involved my department as well as others. I checked the rumor one step above and was given assurance that it was nothing more than rumor. The rumor persisted, and I checked again. It was still claimed to be rumor. It wasn't, and some of the people who trusted me were affected. The higher-level manager who was responsible for providing communications in this instance later excused himself by saying, "Yeah, I knew it, but I didn't have time to get the story to you." Bad management. Bad communications.

People, by their nature, are communicators. We like to talk and to listen. That doesn't mean, however, that we are naturally good at either. In the business scene, communications efforts require that careful attention be paid both to what we hear and to what we say. The sense of responsibility that every manager should have toward his or her subordinates—and superiors—is paramount. The traffic runs both ways.

Managers who communicate well do the following things for the people in their organizations:

○ They give them assurance that what affects them and their jobs will be told to them as quickly and as accurately as possible.
○ They make them feel part of a team—a company.
○ They make them feel respected as individuals.
○ They let them see their manager in the role of a helper on whom they can rely, and not just someone from whom they take direction.

While these benefits are enjoyed throughout the organization, they are particularly important to the middle manager. To bypass the lower-level managers or supervisors is to cheat them of the benefits.

Middle managers who assume communications responsibilities and carry on positive communications practices benefit, too. They enjoy:

- A sense of being in control.
- A sense of perspective—balancing the authority they hold against the obligations they owe.
- Attention from subordinates, who will look to them as the best single source of information.
- Loyalty from those subordinates.
- Effort from subordinates, who will attack their jobs with assurance and enthusiasm and won't have to spend time speculating and gossiping.
- Recognition from superiors who can tell the difference between a smooth operation and one beset with confusion and conflict.

Managers should never wait for the opportunity to communicate. Rather, they should create the opportunity. The time to launch a communications effort is not when there is going to be a layoff, a general increase, a new product introduction, a change in schedules, or a plant shutdown. Begin the process when news is neither so good nor so bad that it *has* to be communicated. Establish the pattern down through the layers of management on a regular basis: Day-to-day information is often as vital as the earth-shattering headline material. Make it habitual. Make it an accepted practice. When the big story breaks, people will expect to hear it from you. Furthermore, they'll believe it!

Part III
Styles, Studies, and Solutions

14

The More We Get Together, the Happier We'll Be

Up to this point, we have attempted to show the nature of discontent among middle managers and the several areas in which changes have to be considered before the problem will be solved. As certainly as all roads lead to Rome, all solutions seem to converge on a single point—the overall style of management. The balance of this short work will offer a simple argument in favor of a participative management style, some suggestions for implementing such a style without the need of adhering to any particular cult of management, and some of the skills managers will have to teach themselves *and* subordinates if they want the style to work for them.

In many respects, adopting a new style or modifying a present style to an improved level is analogous to the golfer who manages to get himself around the course once a week without either (1) being totally embarrassed or (2) playing as well as he wants to. An improved shot here and there would make a considerable difference. If he could just get rid of the slice . . . or the hook. If he could just become consistent with his pitching wedge. He thinks if he concentrates more and tries harder, the problems will be solved. So he concentrates and tries harder, and he plays worse. One part of his game that needed help somehow improves, but the rest of it goes to pieces!

In making these efforts, the golfer is frequently bombarded with much unsolicited and well-intended advice. "Roll the club head over a little, Harry." "Keep your weight on your left foot." "Your shoulder is dropping." "Your stance is too wide." "Your feet aren't lined up properly." If poor Harry tries to pay attention to all this at once, his best bet is to go bowling or buy season tickets at the ballpark. What Harry really needs is a quiet lesson from a professional who knows how to teach. He also has to think differently about the game.

A good pro will take Harry where he is. He'll attempt to correct one thing at a time. Most golf manuals I've ever read will contend that a golf swing is an unnatural combination of body movements. Well, Peter Drucker contended that management is an unnatural act, so the analogy fits. But the golf pro and the management expert will agree on one thing: When you practice the unnatural long enough, it becomes natural—*for you.* In the case of Harry, the golfer, taking on a correct swing would be simpler if he had *never* swung a golf club before; he could learn without first having to *un*-learn. True, too, of the manager; learning and using a style early is simpler than attempting to take on a new approach in midcareer. But in neither case—golf nor management—should we ever conclude that it can't be done.

We said earlier that one of Harry's needs in improving his game was to think differently about it. Let's apply that same idea to management style. Let's apply it specifically to the way style affects middle managers. It makes no difference what style has dominated your company or department before, there are things that can be done to bring about smooth, efficient, and effective changes— changes that will pay off in increased productivity and more cooperation. And that goes in equal doses for the person who manages and the person being managed.

Americans—and Detroiters, in particular—have recently turned their attention to Japanese industry and how that nation seems to be able to produce more goods of higher quality and at lower prices than we can. Tough-minded automobile managers used to shrug off the "Asian menace" with arguments about low-cost labor, U.S. rebuilding of the Japanese industrial complex in the post-World War II period, nonprotective tariffs, and dumping of products to capture markets. All these had some influence, to be sure. And when the oil embargoes and fuel shortages came on the scene, the argument that the product fit the need came front and center. It took nonautomotive people to look more deeply into the situation and come up with still another reason for Japanese success—its management approach.

Some years ago when someone mentioned "Theory Z" to me, I thought it was some cute attempt to hitchhike on Douglas McGregor's Theory X and Theory Y. In a way, it links the two, but more than that, it puts a label on the Japanese approach to management. The subject is dealt with well and in depth by William Ouchi in *Theory Z: How American Business Can Meet the Japanese Challenge,* * so an elaborate discussion of it here is not required. Another new book, *The Art of Japanese Management* by Richard Pascale of Stanford University and Anthony Athos of Harvard, also deals well with it. It is a subject worth considering.

Essentially, the story is one of shared values and mutual interests and concerns between management and the workforce. Japanese management consults and cooperates with the people. American management directs and controls the people. Their management harnesses competence and builds teams. Our management writes policies and issues instructions. The Japanese concept of a manager or supervisor is someone who helps. Our concept is someone who keeps score. The Japanese seem to wash away the lines of hierarchy, while we seem to draw them with indelible ink. Our managers seem to feel an obligation to hand down orders and information from above, and their managers seem to feel obliged to accept input from below.

Pascale, in a recent interview in the *Detroit Free Press*—right on the auto industry's doorstep—describes the Ford Motor Company as illustrative of classic management. It views people instrumen-

* New York: AMACOM, 1981.

tally, according to Pascale, and thinks in terms of top-down flow of ideas and input. Many of the disenchanted managers I know who have left that company tell me much the same thing: Unless you are in full accord with what you are required to do, leaving is the only answer. That mentality was evident among the Ford executives who came to rescue Chrysler in its time of trouble; they carried that style with them. It didn't fit, and it didn't work in countless ways.

That is not to say that directive management styles are impossible to live with. They aren't necessarily reminiscent of sweatshops or chain gangs. They can be civilized and often quite liberal; some managers have learned to be benevolent. They're often very profitable. They're just not interesting and exciting. While that might not mean much at the shop level, where the only reason we have Jake putting on bolts is because we need someone to do it, it doesn't suit the training or the expectations of managers in the middle. They want to think, express their ideas, and—at least once in a while—work on a project that is theirs.

Now there's nothing so special about the Japanese that they can do it and we can't. They're simply willing at times to admit that they don't have all the answers. In this regard, they are partly like many U.S. managers—who don't have all the answers, either. Where the Japanese differ is that they have developed a habit of asking, and we have developed a habit of wrestling with the problems by ourselves.

Several years ago, while I was still in the training activity at Chrysler, we were visited by a group of Japanese automobile dealers. They were sponsored in their tour by Mitsubishi Motors, which was at that time partly owned by Chrysler. Twenty or more of these people came to our conference center, complete with their cameras, tape recorders, and an interpreter. What they wanted to know was how we would recommend that they merchandise used cars. I jokingly told them we were both flattered and astonished that they should ask us *anything* about the car business; they had already demonstrated their mastery in making and in selling them.

They smiled. "You are very kind. We do know much about this. But we want to know more. We think you can tell us much. Then we will do better."

I had some staff members who represented close to 100 years of experience in automotive retailing. They had been prewarned not to approach this meeting as complete experts or to be pedantic in their presentations. They were terrific! We asked, we explained, we exchanged, we learned, and we taught. The interpreter was the busiest person in the room, but the pencils were flying and the note taking was feverish. At the end of the session, the head of the Japanese delegation stood up and made a little speech in which he thanked our members for being so helpful. We, of course, responded in kind, and there was a lot of bowing and smiling. When the Japanese left the center, one of our people said, "Can you imagine a group of *American* dealers doing that? They would have spent the afternoon saying that they already knew this or that, and they would have insisted their way was the best way." Another said, "In spite of the language barrier, I believe we made a contribution. It's nice to be *asked*, and it's nice to be *thanked* that way."

I pondered that session for a long time. I had also been in international conferences in Great Britain, France, Germany, and Latin America. The American management style comes flying through in those encounters. We might listen, but we would also do an inordinate amount of rebutting—insisting that it just wouldn't work that way in New York, Chicago, or Los Angeles. We feel obliged to take over, to demonstrate our superior knowledge. We may be wrong, but we won't let the other guy *think* we're wrong. We tend to be more openhanded, but more closed-minded. The dynamics of our business have been top-oriented for so long that we are uncomfortable in any information interchange that doesn't put us in control. That, it would seem, is the vital difference between Japanese and American approaches to management: We operate, and they cooperate.

If participative management is so effective, why don't we do more of it? The truth is, we have. There are a number of case histories and much well-authenticated research on the subject. The University of Michigan's Institute for Social Research has done some of the best, probably because Rensis Likert was at one time its director. Likert, you may recall, was the behavioral scientist who categorized management styles as four distinct systems. They are:

• *System 1: Exploitative authoritative.* This is the absolute top-down management style. Goals are set, instructions are given, decisions are made at a high level. There is little or no trust of subordinates. Opinions are not sought below. Motivation is a matter of specifically controlled rewards and penalties.

• *System 2: Benevolent authoritative.* This is the paternalistic organization that is friendly, but one never has difficulty telling who the boss is. People might even talk to one another, but it isn't likely that advice would be sought below. Motivation is noticeably reward-centered.

• *System 3: Consultative.* The management is still in control, but people in the lower ranks are given opportunity to express themselves. There is a sense of caution in the communications process, and the upward flow of ideas is more mechanical than natural. The lower one stands in the organization, the less one believes his or her ideas are taken seriously.

• *System 4: Participative.* Communication flows freely in this type of management. There is mutual trust of all people at all levels and a recognition of common purpose. Goals are set, but they are contributed to by managers and workers alike. Rewards still figure in the motivational process, but they are both intrinsic and extrinsic, and power seems to be less at issue than in other styles of management.

Most of us don't know many System 1 managements. It's unlikely that a middle management ever develops in such an environment. We probably recognize or have some well-founded suspicions about some System 2 managements. Many of them grew out of small shops, and the tradition is so ingrained that those who work in them either don't recognize what's happening or don't care. The middle manager in such an enterprise may know that moving up is impossible, but the pay is good, and the position is secure. This type of manager finds his or her independence and recognition in nonjob settings—a church board, a lodge, athletic league, or community service. If the authority is sufficiently benevolent, it probably doesn't matter.

This raises the question, however, about the nature of the authoritarian. I have known many who were delightful people to work with and to be with socially. Most are quick-thinking, self-assured individuals, who have achieved a great deal on their own. They aren't likely candidates for consultation with others; they already have the answers. They develop the habit of coming to their own conclusions, and when they see things to be done, they do them or direct someone else to do them. They're in a hurry. They aren't sinister, but they do have a sense of perfection that can make them critical if things aren't accomplished well or on time. They're likely to pitch in and work anywhere along the line, and they expect others to do the same. In a corporate environment, they're uncomfortable about red tape and protocol.

They function best in situations that are both intimate and totally controllable. Middle management gets in their way. They prefer to give direction—directly. They can survive in a corporate environment if their function is isolated sufficiently to allow them to run a plant as if it were their own or a sales district as though no hierarchy existed above them. They might be middle managers on the corporate organization chart, but in their own territory, they're king!

In countless ways, authoritarians can be fun to work for. The worker who is even the least bit uncertain about how to go about doing something, who wants to contribute but doesn't really know how, may enjoy working under authoritarian leadership. The drive exhibited by the leader can be contagious, and at the end of the day, the crew can look around them and see real accomplishment—more than they could have imagined for themselves. But never try to subdivide the territory, because authoritarians don't work well in pairs. That's why middle managers who report to authoritarians are uncomfortable: They have ideas of their own and want to put them to work.

Now to System 3. If I had to settle for less than the best, I'd opt for System 3. In a sense, it's more understandable and more prevalent than the fully participative management style. It may well be that System 3 is as far as some organizations will ever get. At least it favors the middle manager, even if it doesn't go all the way down into the organization. And it takes a solid middle manager to flourish in this environment—a very real attraction for the person who has confidence and competence. If people listen to you in a System 3 setup, you probably have something to say and say it well.

With System 4, the consultation is extended down through the organization. Likert would add "up and across." In any case, the system is all-encompassing, with involvement at every level. The conventional organizational structure gives way to interrelated groups. This is where the linking-pin concept comes fully into play, with the manager being a subordinate in one group and a leader in the other. Group decision making is the vogue. If you have a stake in the results, you have a voice in the action, and vice versa. Layers of management still exist but are muted by the interrelationship, and the manager receives and gives direction, but without the traditional power application.

System 4 is not for everybody. It certainly requires total commitment by top management in order for it to work. The kind of relinquishing of managerial prerogatives it requires makes it unattractive to many managers. Why be the chairman of a committee when you can be the boss of the gang? A natural reaction to a rather unnatural set of circumstances. However, the values of System 4 are worth considering, because many of the management techniques required to implement the system can be put into effect in any organization, regardless of upper-level support.

Does System 4 work at all? The Michigan Institute for Social Research had the ideal laboratory in which to test its theories when, in 1962, the Harwood Manufacturing Company bought out its leading competitor, the Weldon Manufacturing Company. The two firms had many identical features: Both were manufacturers of pajamas, each had approximately 1,000 employees, and their plants were about the same age. When the acquisition was made, the new owners' intentions were to operate the second company as an autonomous division. Time soon revealed that this wouldn't work, because the two companies operated with two very different management styles. Harwood was run on a participative approach, while Weldon was a traditional authority-obedience operation.

Marrow, Bowers, and Seashore* reported in minute detail the various steps taken and the problems encountered in turning the newly acquired company into a profitable and participative organization. The conditions were perfect for a comparative study—with Weldon a loser and Harwood a winner. Data on efficiency, earnings, operator turnover, and absenteeism reflected the vast difference between the two. In just two years under the new management style, the loser had all but caught up with the leader.

It would be easy to argue that improvement could have taken place under any new system of management. Indeed, the Hawthorne experiment—Elton Mayo's research at the Hawthorne plant of Western Electric Company in the late 1920s—showed that workers change behavior, generally in a positive manner, simply as a result of interest taken in them. You recall the story of the research team providing one group with progressively better working conditions and noting an improvement in productivity. There was also a control group for which nothing was done except having observers from the research group present. That control group's productivity also improved. When asked what could have caused the change, workers simply reported that they thought someone was interested in what they did.

Undoubtedly, that could have accounted for some of the Weldon Company's improved productivity. On the other hand, what about the potential for resentment, the disruptions of loyalties to an older management, the uncertainty over job security? These could have

* *Management by Participation* (New York: Harper & Row, 1967).

subtracted. No, the credit seems due to the move toward a participative management style. But our attention has been riveted on the
line operator; what about the middle manager in this turnaround?

One chapter in the Marrow, Bowers, and Seashore book is contributed by a plant manager of Weldon. He tells of his own first encounter with the new management and the assurances he was given
that he was in charge and that he would be backed by the home
office. I'm sure he wondered how much of this was rhetoric and
how much was real. He tells of the reactions of his own plant management staff. They were well schooled in accepting authority.
They were experienced in plant operation and appreciative of
technology. They were not accustomed to open communications;
they were skeptical of what they heard from above and reluctant to
share information with each other or make suggestions upward.
They were not in the habit of attending and holding meetings or
preparing and receiving reports. And of course, what else does a
participative system live on?

The change process was often painful. Upper-level managers had
to hold themselves back from jumping in and taking over from
lower-level managers. Lower-level managers had to learn to adjust
to working with upper-level managers. Some quit, and some went
through the motions of accepting a new way to work. Some made
the change gracefully and gratefully. Some were perceptive
enough to note that until *they* became comfortable and convinced,
their subordinates were slow to change. The process took time, had
its difficulties; but it was done, *and it worked!*

I am well acquainted with Holland, Michigan—the Tulip Time
town. It was settled back in 1847 by a small band of Netherlanders
looking for a new start in a new land. They operated farms, started
little businesses, built schools and churches, and the town became
attractive to a number of big companies: Chris Craft, Heinz, General Electric, Parke Davis, Beechnut, to name a few. The Dutch
themselves generally were not the movers and the shakers, but they
provided a very sound workforce, and they ran the town, while the
outsiders ran the businesses. It was—and is—a nice arrangement.

One would think that in a community such as this, the big national companies would be the innovators. To be sure, they built plants and presented many opportunities for citizens, and a fair share of Holland's middle management population can trace their lineage back to the pioneers. But the one company that really moved progressively into innovative management methods was a small organization owned by long-time residents of the community. Its name: Donnelly Mirrors, Inc. What put it into national prominence and into a Harvard case study? Participative management.

The company was founded back in 1905. It built mirrors for the then-thriving furniture manufacturing center in Grand Rapids, just 30 miles away. The product was high-quality, with a lot of emphasis on specialties. In the post-World War II period, Donnelly's growth came with the automotive business; it is a major supplier of prismatic and nonprismatic mirrors. Your car probably has one or more Donnelly mirrors on it. They're the parts you never get a recall notice on!

It was a family-owned business. John Donnelly grew up in it. Part of the success of any participative scheme is the direct result of the character of the individual at the top, and John Donnelly is one of those fine people who would make it work. A good businessman, an active community worker, he had a reputation for involvement and integrity. When John said something, people could trust it. I'm sure that when he introduced the new style of management, his colleagues must have said, "If John thinks it will work, it will." He didn't invent participative management, but he took it on as though it were his own.

It began with something called the Scanlon Plan. Joseph Scanlon had been instrumental in initiating a program that involved rank-and-file union members in bailing out a small, struggling steel company in the waning years of the Great Depression. He convinced the company's management that the men would help solve the problem if management would (1) let the workers know what the problems were and (2) demonstrate to them that they would share equitably in the results of improvements. That simple. Management agreed. It worked. Scanlon broadened out to other fields. Donnelly Mirrors got interested.

Variations have occurred over the years in which the program has been in effect at Donnelly, but two key factors hold it together. One is the structure of committees composed of management and nonmanagement people who are elected by their peers. The other is a monthly bonus based on cost savings over an agreed-upon historical base. The formula on which the bonus is computed underwent change only once in an 18-year period.

Results: One product, an automobile mirror, was produced throughout a 20-year period during which the management changes were being introduced and settled. The item grew in dimension—it nearly doubled—improved in quality and field life, and the price was reduced by 25 percent. The market share for the product is now 70 percent. Productivity has grown steadily, and absenteeism runs at about one percent. The good stuff goes up and the bad stuff goes down.

I visited with middle managers at Donnelly to see whether what I read in the papers was true. They assured me it was. I asked how it affected *them*, in the middle. They liked it, but they felt it held the greatest attraction for the top managers and shop-level personnel. That is, the extremes tended to be more involved in it than the middle. Also, it worked better in some departments than in others. Sound familiar? They credited the nature of the people in the community with some of the success—an established work ethic and a respect for authority. However, all new hires are given an orientation program that encourages them to speak up and challenge ideas that appear to be counterproductive. That is equally true of the middle. When asked if they knew any better place to work than where they were, the middle managers laughed. When the top man has a philosophy that's as people-oriented as John Donnelly's, where would there be a better place?

There may not be better places, but there are a growing number of good places. It may not be a whole company you're looking for, just a manager with the self-assurance and wisdom to put such a program to work in his or her department. You'll find managers who work that way in big corporations and in small businesses. It takes just one to start it!

The Weldon-Harwood and Donnelly cases cited above have two common characteristics: They occurred some time ago, and they were successful enough to bear recording. What about up-to-the-minute cases? They're happening all around us. They're happening in different ways, in different industries, with different people, and with a variety of results. The important thing is that management is adopting all or part of the participative approach.

General Motors had a plant in New Jersey that made parts but didn't make money. Under normal operating conditions, the big money-maker might have let things ride, simply for the convenience and control provided by such a plant. But the car bust of the 1980–81 period made them take a second look. They decided to close the place down—to buy the parts rather than make them. The people at that plant had a better idea: If *they* would purchase the shop, would GM continue to buy parts from it? The answer was that GM would as long as it could buy those parts at competitive prices.

The new owners reduced the workforce, cut wages, began doing things differently, and *began making money!* Both quality and quantity of production improved, and they survived the worst downturn in auto business in the past 30 years. How? The management of that plant said *they sat down and talked to people about what needed to be done and what was the best way to do it.* Participative management.

ABEX Corporation is into participative management. It had a foundry in Pennsylvania that was a money loser. The story goes that the president of the company walked in one day, dismissed the plant manager, and called the sales manager in. "You're in charge here," he said. Now, sales managers generally pay no attention to how a plant runs, as long as the plant produces a product that's salable. Here was such a manager with a new job he really didn't know how to do. He didn't pretend. He called in the several managers and supervisors and solicited their ideas. He got them.

Foundries aren't the prettiest places in the world, and only the hardy survive in them. Absenteeism and turnover were problems, and that had an effect on productivity and morale. One thing was evident: The place needed some fixing up. Management closed the shop for three weeks, put in some showers and made other plumbing improvements, painted and cleaned things up, and called people back to work. They held a plant open house; some workers had never had their spouses or families near the shop, and now they were invited to come in. They began doing new things in new ways. Work standards changed, and work attitudes changed. In 18 months, the bottom line had turned from a loss to a profit. How? *Someone asked someone else* how he or she might like to see things happen.

The Dana Corporation advertises the fact that it talks to people in its business. It does very nicely—in part, as a result of that talk. Sperry advertises the fact that it listens to customers, to the public, and to its employees. Sperry, in fact, regularly makes the news with its training programs on listening. I might have thought it was all public relations, but I have lunch regularly with one of the firm's middle managers, and he says it's all true. It has become a very productive and profitable way of life for Sperry.

The automotive industry, known for its top-down management style, came on hard times in 1980–81. Chrysler, in order to keep afloat, went not only to the government for loan guarantees but also to the UAW for concessions. It got them, but it also got Doug Fraser, president of the union, on its board of directors. As 1982 opened, Ford and General Motors sought an early reopening of contract talks with the same union. Their concern: Wages and benefits paid to U.S. workers prevent the domestic companies from competing effectively with Japanese imports. They got concessions, but they'll ultimately get something else—worker representation on their boards and a demand to be heard from below.

What does this mean to the middle managers? They may end up as watchers while top management and labor work out schemes to save corporations and jobs. Or—and one hopes this will be the case—they may end up as the proper intermediaries between the factory floor and the executive suite. It's a challenge to be met. The first step can take place in a single department, with middle managers managing one another properly and readying themselves to take their proper roles. When they can prove themselves capable of implementing the communications process at that level, they will have earned the larger assignment.

15

It May Look Good on Paper,
But It Just Won't Work in My Business

The story is told of the aeronautical engineers who were given all the data on the bee. Their conclusion: "It is impossible for such a thing to fly." Then one of those little "nonflyers" must have *crawled* out onto the golf course last summer to sting me!

It is almost axiomatic that nothing will work if the person in charge of the project says it won't. It's a good thing that bees are not the responsibility of the aeronautical engineers—the first one would never have been made. So it is with the installation of a new or modified management style. If you think it will work, it *might*. If you think it won't, it *can't*. But there's a hidden message in all this: *The manager who says it won't work in his or her situation is the manager about whom subordinate managers complain!* Thomas Edison is credited with saying, "Show me a thoroughly satisfied man, and I will show you a failure."

Opening up the management style has obvious risks, but risks need not be gambles. To say that introducing a participative or consultative management style would never work in your business is to be blind to the possibilities. The benefits to be derived by the manager are even greater than those to be derived by the subordinates. More than that, here is an opportunity to go after the big results with only piece-by-piece investment of time and trouble. There is even an emergency hatch or a safety net: If it doesn't work, go back to your tired, old way of doing business.

Ponder this: Some anonymous writer once put down these steps to achievement—"I won't. I can't. I don't know how. I wish I could. What is it? I think I might. I might. I think I can. I can. I will. I did!" Go about halfway back in that string, and you'll find the turning point: "What is it?" Whenever I have met a real skeptic about the potential of participative or consultative management, it generally turned out that the individual wasn't quite sure what it entailed. Or if the knowledge was there, it was a case of feeling that getting into the newer style would be terribly difficult. It is if you make it so; it needn't be.

You can call it participative, consultative (even though the Likert forces would discriminate between the two), organization development, management by objectives, team building, open management, or many other labels. It is *not* democratic, management by consensus, or by committee. It isn't, as someone once put it, letting the inmates run the asylum. The important thing is not to get too wrapped up in procedures and jargon. Look at it in its simplest form—working together to get the job done.

By whatever name it goes under, the participative management style is built on a communications process in which those affected have the opportunity to express themselves and share in the molding of courses of action. At times, the process is a group affair—meetings with other managers to hammer out departmental issues. At other times, it may be a simple one-on-one exchange between a manager and a subordinate. It may, and probably will, involve written communications—planning and reporting. *It is a process that is manager-controlled, but not manager-dominated.*

Although it plays positively to the feelings of people, it focuses carefully on business objectives and the efforts required to achieve those objectives. It elevates rather than subdues those who are a part of it. It provides the manager a great opportunity to supervise at close range without the sense of meddling or spying. It gives the subordinate an opportunity to reveal talents that might otherwise be overlooked. It lets the manager compare the capabilities of subordinates, and it lets subordinates compare themselves with their peers.

Participative management provides a natural avenue for the delegation of responsibilities. It also highlights individual accountability, because it openly balances responsibility with authority. It makes clear the nature and extent of management support, and it explains why such support is given or withheld. It multiplies output without similarly multiplying effort and frustration. It refines and develops all who are involved in the process. *It answers every single complaint ever put forth by an unhappy middle manager!*

Many of my peers in the training business will drum me out of the corps for saying this: Don't worry so much about pushing the system too far down in the organization. It will get there. Don't feel you have to obliterate the organization chart or disrupt protocol. They will tend to blur by themselves. Don't feel that you have to broadcast the good news about what's happening in your department. It will get around somehow. Don't feel that the entire style has to be in place before any part of it will work. It grows by itself. But don't believe for one minute that it will happen just because you want it to; you have to work for it. Someone once said that we should take our cue from the woodpecker—use our head and keep pecking away.

In the previous chapter, we mentioned several cases in which the participative style worked. Two of them were quite different in their origins, and they were *very* different in the way they went together. In the Harwood-Weldon case, the CEO of the takeover company was a student of management style who called in consultants to implement the change. In the Donnelly case, the CEO was an interested and concerned businessman who began with a germ of an idea, risked using it, and refined the process as he went along. He used consultants whose ideas seemed to expand on what he was doing. The first was a textbook case, and the second was a case that made the textbooks.

That's fine, but *you* work for a biggie like a major steel company or a giant energy company. Your management would frown on it. Or you work in a small company where the management is so top-down that you'd be considered avant-garde if you tried something that looked like cooperation. Consider this: In companies where this kind of participative management is *not* used, where people are viewed as elements in the production process but not stakeholders in it, where all that matters is results—*such management isn't paying much attention to you, anyhow!* By introducing participative techniques, all you're really doing is rearranging the environment within your own control. Unless you make a big fuss over what you're doing, or unless you do it so badly that you put the whole department into a turmoil, you'll be a success before anyone upstairs catches on!

Another argument we've heard about not going into a participative type of management style is that subordinates won't take to it. Well, that may be true if you have been such a dominant manager that your subordinates will react to any changes by thinking it's time to call in the guys with the white coats. But if you *were* that type, you wouldn't be reading a book of this sort, or you wouldn't have kept at this one this long. The archetype of the dominant manager, indeed, is the kind of person who doesn't read books at all: They get in the way of hard-knuckle operators. Most managers have risen through the work ranks to the supervisory ranks or have had equivalent schooling and realize that if people under their control won't move into a participative or consultative style, the problem lies deeper. The subordinate who *can't* needs development, and the subordinate who *won't* needs a trip to the analyst or a pass to the main gate.

Usually the argument that subordinates won't take to participative management is made by a manager who has never even tested the idea. Sometimes it takes the subordinate to make the first move. Often the change-over from authoritarianism to participation is like the born-again idea—rapid and dramatic. Once used, the idea always sticks.

One of the more pleasant and rewarding assignments I had in the Chrysler training activity was working with classes of dealers' sons and daughters in a very ambitious and concentrated conference program. We would host several groups of 20 to 25 students each year for a four-week, eight-hour-a-day instructional session. Here were young future managers of automobile dealerships. Their concerns about having jobs or ultimately succeeding in them were minimal—their fathers *owned* the businesses. Their concerns about having something to say about what they did *right now* were maximal—their fathers *ran* the businesses. *And their fathers had neither a sense of participative management nor trust in the competence of their offspring!* Of course not. Here were entrepreneurs—doers, achievers—people who knew the business but were skeptical that the kids could take over and repeat the success.

I used to take delight in saying to the young men and women toward the end of their stay at the training center, "Don't go home and tell your Dad that you know more about the business than he does. Just go home and tell him you're ready to show him how much you *do* know. Ask him for a chance. Prove a few things *quietly*. Ask him for advice once in a while and give him advice in return. It'll work out." Parents would come in for a graduation celebration, and *every* time, one of the dealers would say, "Johnnie was home for a weekend two weeks ago, and I get the impression that you people have taught him a lot. He wants to take over one of the departments. Do you think he's ready?" "Only if you are," was my standard answer.

Did it work? I used to get into some of those dealerships later on. One young lady, whose father probably thought she was still his little girl, took over the management of the office in a multimillion dollar operation. One young man proved himself so well that his father opened another store and put him in charge of it. Another took over the management of the business when his father became ill, and his Dad never did get back in the driver's seat. *Subordinates are ready when you are!*

One of the deeper sources of reluctance on the part of a manager is the thought that by going to a participative management style and sharing responsibility and authority, his or her own authority will be eroded. If that's the case, one question deserves to be asked: Is the source of your authority your expertise in this business or just your position? If the answer is that your expertise is what counts, then you can be sure that subordinates will continue to accord you respect and authority—willingly!

The interesting appeal of a participative management style for the manager is that the style becomes a showcase for expertise. The way you conduct meetings and counseling sessions shows one side of your talent. The manner in which you exercise judgments, delegate responsibilities, arbitrate differences, and distribute rewards shows still another. Then, too, there is the element of courage and stability that is revealed in the manager who is willing to take ideas, evaluate, and support them. The more open style puts you where others can observe your expertise and your character, while the highly directive style separates you from others, hides your real qualities.

Unlike the line in the old song, "Wishing will make it so," wishing won't carry you very far in implementing the management style that will attract and motivate middle managers under your control. It will take some know-how and some work. It isn't impossible, and it needn't be done in one major program. If you aren't doing any participative managing now, are doing a little and want to do more, or are doing quite a bit of it and want to do it better, here are some easy-to-follow directions for getting it on track. Please note that the intention here is to lay out a pattern to follow. Full explanations and helpful materials for implementing the steps can be found in later chapters.

• Begin with the attitude that every manager or supervisor under your direction is a Theory Y individual. Simply stated, that means that each of your subordinates has the *potential* for being an achievement-oriented, self-starting, and hard-working person like yourself.

• Do a preliminary, thoughtful evaluation of what you might expect from each individual—where your best support will come from, and where your problems might arise.

• Make a list of developmental needs that will have to be cared for on an individual basis and on a group basis. For instance, who communicates well and who doesn't, and who seems to be a good problem solver and who isn't? You will be faced with bringing certain individuals up to standard before they can become truly contributory.

• Do a quick review of motivational theory. It will not only strengthen your resolve to go on with the opening of your management style, but it will also make you more articulate in its defense. You may even be called on to teach a little of it to those on your staff who have never been exposed to it. (A chapter on this follows.)

• Review the principles of discussion leadership and one-to-one counseling. While these skills may have nothing to do with the core concepts of your business, they have everything to do with how well you facilitate group processes. For one thing, you'll find yourself doing more probing and listening than ever before, and it won't hurt to know how to do it better. (Chapters on meetings and counseling follow.)

• Begin consultation with one staff member on one item of business he or she has responsibility for. Pick a problem or a program where you would feel comfortable allowing the subordinate latitude in expression and in subsequent action. ("What do you know. The boss asked me how I'd like to handle the job, then let me go ahead and do it *my way!*")

• Ditto, the rest of the group—one at a time.

• Identify areas in which two or more managers on the staff have interlinking interests and responsibilities. Pick one you've been wanting to change in some way. Bring the interested parties together and play referee.

• Select problems in which all members of the staff can make contributions. Budgets, forward plans, special promotions, or campaigns—all are natural group activities. You may be interested to observe the trading that takes place if you haven't already done some of this.

• Wherever you discover difficulties in the process, look for areas of incompetence that may be the cause of such difficulties. You may have to teach—in a group or in a private session—such things as proper attitudes, cooperation, how to attack problem solving, what it means to set goals, how to present ideas, and how to pin down the essentials in a report. (Chapters on these also follow.)

• Beware of giving false impressions. Not everything in your business is subject to group process and shared decisions. Some things will inevitably come from above, and some things have no room for choice in content or application. Nobody ever resented taking tight direction from a manager who really has to give it.

• Keep working at the process until *it* works.

The process, once attempted, will work in your favor. It will also gain quick acceptance by your subordinates. That's because they will see that you are not treating them, as was suggested earlier in this book, as mere underlings, who were hired to follow directions, do the kinds of things you don't like to do, or do the kinds of things you can't do very well. By the simple act of involving your managers and supervisors in the *meaningful* parts of the work—planning, deciding, choosing courses of action, making the action produce results, and sharing in the fun of achieving—you are letting them live up to their own expectations of a managerial role. Further, your own rewards will become immediately evident:

○ Relationships will improve on a broad scale.

○ Concerns will become less personal, more work-directed.

○ Objectives will be met in terms of quality, quantity, and time.

○ Your own work will take on a different tone—with more time spent in being creative and less time spent in unbuttoning problems and adjudicating complaints.

In the process, you might rid yourself of some of your own middle management concerns and confusions. Work that's properly done cures a lot of ills!

16

Blue Sky and Solid Ground

With most managers, a little motivational theory goes a long way. I understand that. But I don't agree that we can function intelligently and effectively with people if we have no respect for motivational theory at all. In earlier chapters, I alluded to several of the key influences in modern motivational thinking and writing. Now it's time for us to take a quick, hard look at a few of the more dominant points of view from which *this* point of view is formed. If you are a true student of the subject, you'll likely consider this short rendering of theories and their applications inadequate and perhaps less than reverent. If you are not such a student, you may find it helpful in discovering the reasons why what you do with middle managers a step below you—and a step above—works or doesn't work.

Some years ago, a high-level union official said of the motivational theories that they were abstract concepts . . . not relevant, pertinent, or meaningful . . . masquerades of scientific research . . . unadulterated nonsense that didn't fit in the real world. His remarks represent the point of view that manager-subordinate relationships are, by nature, adversary. If we begin there and are willing to go no further, then to discuss the theories is a waste of time. But if we believe, or even *hope*, that I-win/you-lose attitudes are not only old-fashioned but unworkable today, we deserve to explore the behavioral sciences just a little.

When I side with those who say that a little theory goes a long way, I mean that I object to making any theory a religion to which I bow and scrape. That's where some organizational specialists and human resource developers have stubbed their toes; by being carried away with some current and fashionable cult, they have come off like eggheads and have lost credibility. It is entirely possible for us to explore a little blue sky and yet remain on terra firma. Let's try.

First, let's disassociate behavioral science from the post-World War II surge of human relations theory. That movement was aimed at making people feel better, on the assumption that they would then work harder. Behavioral science is keyed to the concept that if we make people work effectively, they'll feel better. Let's also disassociate behavioral science from manipulative psychology. If we believe that our subordinates are puppets, who move because we pull certain strings, then we are tangled in the wrong strings. Behavioral science takes a look at motivation as an inner force that is released, not as an outer force that is applied. Some difference!

For centuries, thinkers explored the human mind and its influences. Philosophers played with ideas, formed conclusions, gathered adherents. Psychology was born. Freud, Jung, and others whose names are always mentioned as pioneers in the field were, in reality, fairly recent—born in the 19th century, they worked in the 20th. So we really didn't know much or do a lot about behavior until our own times. It's currently a full-time preoccupation for many. What's important for those of us who have to work at other things is to be able to pick the more meaningful and more readily applicable ideas.

The Hawthorne experiments, which began in 1927, are considered by many to be the genesis of behavioral science in industry. Elton Mayo and his associates studied work groups, initially hoping to find the relationship of work environment to monotony and fatigue—ultimately, to productivity. To their surprise, they came upon new findings: They discovered that physical factors in the workplace played a lesser role than the attention given to workers on the job. They also learned that workers were not simply individuals within a group, but that groups took on personalities of their own. The interdependency, the shared interests and values, and the members' internal regulation of one another's behavior became the more significant findings. In fact, those studies revealed that management's old belief that it ran the show was more imagined than real.

The studies were ill-timed, in the sense that what was learned came out during the days of the Great Depression. ("So, who cares what people think or feel—they have a job, don't they?") But as times improved, the Hawthorne experiments kept nagging at some of the more forward-thinking managers and students of management. More and more attention was paid to worker feelings and reactions. Some of it even spilled over on middle management!

At about the same time the Hawthorne experiments were taking shape, E. L. Thorndike was exploring what seemed to be an unrelated field—learning. His concern was what made one child learn and another not learn, even when they were in similar environments. After considerable experimentation, it was concluded that children performed best when they sensed a reward for good performance or a penalty for poor performance. It was a simple equation of the unpleasant versus the pleasant—*losses versus gains*. The theory became known as the Empirical Law of Effect.

Consider that for just a moment. Isn't that what turns you on and off? Each of us wants to gain or keep from losing. Apply that to the many complaints of the middle manager. He or she wants to gain materially—suitable pay and benefits. And the emotional rewards, too—sense of worth, feeling of accomplishment, opportunity to grow and be appreciated. The list goes on and on, but it boils down to rewards and penalties, gains and losses.

Abraham Maslow, in the mid-1950s, took the matter of rewards and penalties a step further with his now-famous "hierarchy of needs." It links personality with motivation in a very systematic way. It goes like this:

- People's needs are arranged in five ascending steps. These needs begin with *physiological* needs—food, clothing, shelter, sex—anything required to support life and maintain the race. The next step up constitutes *safety* needs—to preserve whatever one has. The next covers a sense of *belonging*—social needs. Above that is the need for *esteem*—ego satisfaction. Finally, on the top step, is the need for *self-actualization*—achievement.

• Maslow's contention was that people are not likely to seek the goal above until the step they are on is suitably satisfied. Hence, it is safe to say that once a goal is reached, it is no longer a motivator.

• All human beings have the capacity to climb the several steps. Those who do demonstrate emotional maturity; those who don't demonstrate immaturity.

If, as Maslow pointed out, people move from one motivational level to another, consider where the average middle manager stands on the scale. Middle managers are generally individuals with tenure, have better-than-average compensation and benefits, and enjoy relative security, in that they feel their personal competence justifies their roles. To them, the physical and security needs are muted, if not wholly satisfied. Their interests lie above, in the areas of wanting to belong and individual recognition. Belong to what? To your managerial staff. Recognition for what? For their abilities to make contributions to the thoughtful processes for which management is responsible. And then there is the level of self-actualization—the sense of achievement. That's ultimately on their minds, too.

It may be difficult to see the line worker in this context, but it should require no imagination-stretching to see the middle manager in it. And here's another clue: Maslow contended that all of us have the capacity to climb in the hierarchy of needs, with those who *do* demonstrating emotional maturity and those who *don't* demonstrating immaturity. Doesn't that tell us something about the middle managers under our supervision? It tells me that the dissident may be ever so much more valuable to the enterprise than the complacent person who is willing to accept tasks unquestioningly or without offering any suggestion about how tasks should be performed. As you open your management style to allow for participation, you'll get a most interesting reading on those who surround you. Build on the strengths of those who are in a rush to get somewhere, and you'll get somewhere yourself!

Douglas McGregor is a name found frequently in literature on management and human behavior. His *Human Side of Enterprise** put new terminology into the field: Theory X and Theory Y. McGregor chose as his starting point two assumptions about people at work: The conventional assumption that people didn't like to work, needed prodding, and preferred security was laid against the behavioral assumption that people did enjoy doing things, were self-starters, and liked to achieve. Note that these were assumptions drawn to highlight the study of behavior at work, not strict definitions of two distinct kinds of people.

What I learn from McGregor is that we, the managers, actually cause subordinates to fit each pattern. If we manage people as though they don't like to work, need prodding, and so forth, we will find them living up to the expectation. Conversely, if we manage people with the underlying thought that they could be self-directing and responsible, they will prove to be such. Of course you know people who seem to fit the Theory X pattern: Their work experiences have put them there. There's more to Theory X and Theory Y than what has been written here, but even this little bit gives us a springboard to better understanding. What it suggests is that unless we give people a chance to stand on their own two feet, take part in their own destiny, and demonstrate their capabilities, we will forever be stuck with the chore of giving direction and exercising control.

The middle management segment of the workforce is the perfect place to do this. Middle managers are where they are because somewhere along the line they have demonstrated abilities and attitudes that have been thought to be positive and productive. We

* New York: McGraw-Hill, 1960.

create managers from exceptional sales representatives, production workers, specialists in technology, accountants, and so forth. We take them from the top of one pile and put them at the bottom of another. We take them out of an environment in which they feel comfortable and put them into another in which they feel threatened. They may require a lot of direction and control at the outset of their managerial experience, but they also require a growing acknowledgment of their capabilities and a demonstration that their value will rise in direct proportion to their ability to take independent action.

Josten's—known everywhere for its jewelry and incentive awards—is a multidivisional organization. People are constantly moving up in the several sales organizations. Field offices are everywhere in the country. The firm's sales managers must assume responsibilities quickly and operate autonomously. What do you suppose their first managerial training program focuses on? They are told at the very outset that they are *managers—in charge*—and that their management relies on them. The new career begins with confidence building and support. That's taking Theory Y out of the closet and putting it in the display window!

Middle managers need to know that the roles they play are not mere tasks to which they've been assigned, but responsibilities for taking charge. They have to be made to feel that their opinions are valuable and should be expressed. They should be managed as Theory Y people, even if you have some questions about whether or not they truly qualify for the honor. If you don't, they will be self-fulfilling prophesies—in need of direction, control, and prodding. You'll never get the job done that way, and middle managers who are managed that way are a constant source of irritation to their bosses and to themselves.

We also mentioned earlier the ideas of Frederick Herzberg. His contribution to the literature on behavioral science was the neat discrimination between things that satisfy and things that dissatisfy people at work. They deserve another look:

○ Things that dissatisfy are company policies and administration, supervision, working conditions, interpersonal relations, salaries, status, job security, and personal life.
○ Things that satisfy are achievement, recognition, work itself, responsibility, advancement, and growth.

Herzberg's findings weren't based on supposition or prejudgment. He simply asked a lot of people two basic questions: Can you describe when you felt good about your job? Can you describe when you felt bad about your job? People felt good when they were working, doing something worthwhile, getting recognized for it, being given opportunity to grow and advance. What was it we said middle management people really wanted? The *very same things!* But too often they don't get them; the simplest, most productive motivators are withheld, while corporate leaders throw money at the problem.

Rensis Likert, also mentioned previously, came to similar conclusions with independent research and analysis. He went beyond the individual and explored the makeup of the organization. His concepts include:

• The linking-pin principle—the overlapping character of the business organization, in which the leader of one group is the subordinate in another—highlights the importance of mutual goals and sharing in communication and decision making.

• The interaction-influence principle. This suggests that managers have *formal* authority over subordinates, but their *real* authority is subject to how much authority their subordinates *allow* them to have. Stated another way, managers influence subordinates in direct relation to the influence those subordinates exert upward. *And* the amount of influence a manager is perceived to have *upward* and *laterally*—with his or her bosses and other upper-level managers—has a halo effect on the amount of influence he or she can exert *downward*. Think of great leaders you have known, and they'll fit this pattern nicely.

• The supportive-relationship principle. Unless leadership is trusted and displays trust in return, relationships tend not to be supportive of one another. When people can openly communicate ideas and feelings, they perceive support. Such perceived support makes for greater respect and cooperation.

Likert, of course, is best known for his four systems of management style previously covered. What is interesting about his work and that of the University of Michigan's Institute for Social Research is the dogged testing of these several theories in actual work settings.

Another well-known contribution to the lore of behavioral science is the Blake-Mouton Managerial Grid. It presents graphically the two seemingly irreconcilable points of view: concern for people and concern for production. On a vertical scale is laid the concern for people, which portrays the people-centered manager as being one who pays attention to the needs of individuals for satisfying relationships, comfortable and friendly work atmospheres, and so forth. On the horizontal scale is laid the concern for production, which portrays the production-centered manager as one who seeks efficiency in the operation by arranging conditions in such a way that human elements interfere as little as possible. From these two opposites come, in Blake and Mouton's view, a third approach: work accomplished by committed people who have a common stake in the organization's purpose, which leads to relationships of trust and respect.

The span goes from "country club management" to "task management" to "team management." It would be a good idea for the manager who has not confronted the grid concept to do so, because it allows a manager to perform self-evaluation in a very succinct way.

All of the above concepts in the behavioral sciences have been broadly published and widely taught in schools of business administration. One of the problems the old-timer in management may have with younger, recently educated subordinates is that they are informed about these ideas and use them as a yardstick to measure their bosses. I am constantly amazed at how few upper middle managers know much, if anything, about behavioral science research and reporting. Even if a management tends to consider such material bookish and unworkable, it owes itself an opportunity to read or hear well-informed people discussing it in a practical sense. Having done so, it's unlikely that wholesale rejection of these findings will continue to linger.

As we look back over the several points of view set forth by the experts, we can't escape recognizing the fact that, however differently these theories and principles have been stated, they all seem to lead to a single conclusion: Respect, trust, and responsibility granted will bring respect, trust, and responsibility in return. If we are to achieve objectives, we have to include subordinates in their formulation—make those objectives theirs as well as ours. If we are to achieve support from below, we must provide it from above. If we expect people to be self-starting and self-fulfilling, we have to use that as our standard at the outset.

We must bear in mind that the scholars who gave us these interesting theories and points of view were convinced that managerial behavior of the sort recommended could span all the way from the very top of an organization down to the lowliest job in the company. And that makes the complaints of the middle manager all the more astonishing. It can't span the whole distance if it never gets going in the middle! Or perhaps it's more truthful to say that we *assume* it will happen in the middle, so we pay little or no attention to making it happen. We *assume* managers manage managers as they themselves would like to be managed. But, in truth, it happens only sometimes, and sometimes never!

A final thought on theory, then we'll leave it. I learned a great lesson on the subject in a nonbusiness setting, when our minister preached a sermon on traditions. "Traditions," he said, "have an interesting attraction for people, and in times like these when traditions are so frequently being challenged and discarded, many people become quite upset to see the traditions they have cherished tarnish or vanish. Consider this: A tradition that has merit will survive. A tradition without merit will ultimately fall, and in its place will rise another." I have since substituted the word "theory" for the word "tradition."

Some of the theories I have described in this chapter have survived a long time in an age when new ideas constantly come and go. Theories that survive are either those that were born in the mind of their articulator and tested in the workplace for verification, or they are observations repeatedly made in the workplace and then chronicled by their sponsor. They don't hang around if they don't hold water. These have been around a long time and have gone through some severe testing. I said at the outset that I would deal with them briefly and without undue awe; the fact that they make sense when laid together is proof enough for me.

But these theories require effort in order to work. The following chapters highlight some of the things good managers have to do if they are to succeed at working effectively on a day-to-day basis with their middle management personnel.

Part IV
Aptitudes, Attitudes, and Actions

17

The Best Conversations Require Two People and One Interesting Subject

If you have agreed to this point that participative management can be employed even on a limited basis—not requiring total organizational restructuring, but on a single-department level—you have taken the first important step in solving the middle management riddle. If you have also concluded that it is necessary to see your subordinate managers and supervisors as Theory Y people—whether you are totally comfortable with the idea or not—you have taken the second important step. Keep thinking that when you are dealing with managers, you are dealing with achievers like yourself, and that they need room to prove themselves.

To implement your resolve to move ahead, there are two key skills you'll have to sharpen and develop for yourself. The first is your ability to counsel and coach, and the second is your ability to hold productive staff meetings. My own recommendation is that you begin your move toward a more open management style with a series of one-on-one conferences with individual staff members. That way their concerns about participating will be allayed, and you can make your mistakes a bit more privately. We'll discuss some of the cardinal points of coaching and counseling in this chapter and tackle the meeting skills in the next.

Bear in mind that when a manager sits down with a subordinate, the first thing he or she must have in mind is an objective. What will this meeting—even if it is intended to last only five or ten minutes—accomplish for both parties? When you summon one of your managers or supervisors to your office, or when you drop in on theirs, something productive must occur. If you have been a directive manager to this point, your subordinate will probably guess that he or she is being confronted to be given orders. That may be the first hurdle you'll have to jump. It may require several encounters before the subordinate really believes that something different is taking place. So your first step is to have an objective in mind, and the second is to be quick in making it clear to the other party what your objective is:

- "Mary, I know you're going to start preparing for the upcoming sales meeting, and I thought we might talk for a few minutes about what our real problems are and how you intend to handle them."
- "Sam, your department has had a lot of absenteeism in the past few weeks. My guess is that you've already looked into that. I thought we might talk about that for just a little while. Maybe you have some suggestions for turning that situation around."

In the first opener, you've done three things for Mary. The first is an expression of your awareness of a responsibility she has. The second is an invitation to explore the core problems that need attention. The third is your suggestion that she, with you, will have a say in what shape the meeting will take. Overall, you have made a statement concerning the objective of your meeting.

In the second opener, you've done a few things for Sam. First, you've let Sam know that *you* know that he has a problem. Second, you've put him in a position of having to provide you with whatever information he has on the background of the problem. You have also announced your intentions to participate with him in defining and solving the problem. Again, you have made a statement of objective.

It's important to initiate one-on-one discussions this way. The early statement of an objective does two very vital things: It sets a *direction* and puts a *limitation* on the discussion. If more meetings began this way, there would be fewer digressions and more concentration on key issues. There would also be less time spent, and that's an advantage no manager would brush aside; much time is wasted in conversations that don't *get* to the point and don't *keep* to the point. You'll never be interpreted as rude or abrupt if, when the conversation gets off track, you say, "We'll make time to talk about that later in the day, Jack; right now, we should be concerned about putting *this* matter to rest."

If discussions of the sort we're talking about are preliminary, you may initiate them without much prior notice. If, on the other hand, they're subjects on which preparations should have taken place, it could be to your advantage and your subordinate's as well to set a time allowing at least the gathering of papers and the collection of thoughts. Participatory sessions should be focused on productivity in an environment that is reasonably stressless. To pop a meeting on a subordinate who may not be wholly prepared is to subvert the process. Save spur-of-the-moment meetings until after the idea of free-flow involvement is well seated; it is still a manager's prerogative to expect preparation and ready response, and this is a subtle form of discipline you can hold in reserve.

If you stick to your objective of exploring with the subordinate his or her ideas on a subject, learn not to interrupt or disagree until very late in the process. Interruptions and challenges do more to turn off the creative flow than anything else. It would be best to follow the principal rules of brainstorming—encourage ideas, deem no idea worthless, stimulate add-ons and adjustments by the originator, iron out the wrinkles later. You may have once been in the subordinate role yourself, offering suggestions that were maybe just in the formative stage, only to be stopped before the ideas could be refined. Your conclusion in such a situation was that it would have been better not to have opened your mouth in the first place. Don't turn the tables on your subordinate manager or supervisor if you expect the participative process to succeed.

At this point, the burden of discipline is totally on the manager who is seeking to involve the subordinate. It isn't easy. I have sat with subordinates who were groping for thoughts and expressing poorly formed suggestions. To have jumped in to criticize or correct would have been self-defeating. On one occasion I recall saying, "Maybe we got into this before you had a chance to think it through. Suppose we take a crack at it after lunch." When you take your participant off the hook, at least early in the game, you have indicated that you're more interested in getting real input than you are in showing your power. If, on the other hand, you feel that ample preparation time has been granted, you have a perfect right to take a sterner hand. It's a judgment call that requires lots of practice, and it will rely heavily on your appraisal of the individual's capacity to handle your demands.

Your role as a manager exploring ideas with subordinate managers is one of knowing how to stimulate input and keep it on track. The process depends greatly on questions—how they're constructed and presented. In any coaching or counseling session, managers should try to:

• Ask open questions. These are questions to which the answer must be more than yes or no. An open question might be, "What do you believe has caused the absenteeism lately?" A closed question might be, "Have you looked into the reasons for absenteeism?" The open question obviously will produce more conversation.

• Ask questions that encourage creative responses. This prevents getting textbook answers. "We've done this program year after year . . . pretty much the same. If you could do it differently—no holds barred—what kind of changes would you want to make?" That frees the responder to break loose with new contributions.

• Ask questions in such a way that the subordinate doesn't feel threatened. Keep the conversation away from sounding like, "I ask, you answer." Your purpose is not to quiz, but to discover and develop ideas that lead to decisions.

• Pursue responses with other questions. "You mentioned one

thing you felt would work. How would you go about doing that if we were to agree to try it?"

• Withhold judgment until the latter part of any session, so that the free flow of dialog isn't interrupted. Then lead the judgment rather than pronounce it. "I see some problems with what you have in mind. Do you?" That will kick off further exchange that would clarify the position and lead to confirmation or rejection, as the case may be.

Participative sessions between the manager and the subordinate will take on many shapes and sizes. Some may become coaching sessions, in which the manager attempts to help the subordinate sharpen a skill. Some may become counseling sessions, in which attitudinal changes are sought. Others may center on work planning, goal setting, problem solving, or organizational adjustments. A few will take half an hour or less, and a few may involve half a day or more. A cardinal rule to follow is never to confuse instruction with discipline or giving orders with exchanging ideas. Separate them whenever possible, because when you don't, the subordinate is correct in thinking, "When I admit I don't know how to do something, first I get chewed out, then I get help. And when I'm asked for my opinion, I always end up doing it the boss's way, anyhow."

Another thing managers should learn to do if they are to make any kind of participative effort work is to take a chance on the subordinate's recommended course of action. His or her way may not be your way, but if it will work, so what? As long as it isn't illegal, against policy, dangerous to life and limb, counterproductive, or excessively costly, give it a try. Most middle management complaints are lodged against just such nitpicking by bosses. Getting the job done is the ultimate goal, and if it's done differently than the way you had in mind, who cares?

I used to have a supervisor whose responsibility it was to schedule conferences and map out instructor travel plans. We would go over the forward plan at stated intervals for final approval. Commonly I would already have some parts of the schedule in mind, and then the supervisor would present his version of it. Sometimes it differed with my preconception by 180 degrees. If it covered all the bases and could be defended as a workable plan, I signed off on it. If it didn't, it got changed. What I used to have to admit often was that he was the one who had worked at the plan and had to make it work for him; all I had done was given it a prejudiced thought or two. That's what subordinate managers and supervisors are supposed to do—keep their bosses from making mistakes!

Every participative session should end on a note of commitment to meet a certain objective, to apply a certain skill, to take on a specific attitude, or to follow a definite course of action. To be sure, a single session may not bring you to a final solution, but it should close on what happens next. We couldn't make a firm decision on the issue today, so we'll meet again on it tomorrow. That's a commitment to a course of action. Ultimately, we'll arrive at the point where there will be no tomorrow, and the course of action is set today. But at each step of the involvement, both parties leave the session with a knowledge of what happens next as a result of what just happened now.

No small part of the manager's commitment is to indicate support for the subordinate. "Go to it. I'm behind you" should be expressed or strongly implied. Only the brave are willing to take on their own program of action without the boss's concurrence. Only the foolish will do so with the thought that the boss is waiting in the wings to have the last laugh. If it doesn't work out right, it's the manager's responsibility to point out what went wrong and to get things back on track. But, please, suppress the urge to say, "I told you so!"

As a sort of role play to illustrate what has been said above, let's take fragments of the conversation between the manager and Mary and between the manager and Sam. Wherever possible, notes will be given to highlight the techniques involved.

You're a sales director. Mary Parker is your manager of sales services. She coordinates meetings, oversees training, and handles field communications. She is now in her second year on the job.

Last year's major sales meeting was put together by you and other staff members, but Mary now knows what happens and what seems to be expected, so she is assuming the full responsibility this year. The date has been set, but planning is just beginning. You drop by Mary's office early one morning and say, "I've been thinking about the upcoming sales meeting, Mary. If you can arrange to spend an hour or so on it this morning, let's meet in my office about 9:30." Mary says she'll be there. At 9:30 sharp, she appears in your doorway.

You: Mary, I know you're going to start preparing for the sales meeting, and I thought we might talk for a few minutes about what our real problems are and how you intend to handle them. (Mary knows the job is hers and that she is expected to contribute her ideas.)

Mary: Well, so far, we've made reservations at the Greenway Inn and checked out its meeting rooms. You've held meetings there before, so you know what they are.

You: It's a nice place. And I'm glad you've made those arrangements. At least that's out of the way. What thoughts have you had about the program?

Mary: I thought you'd set that up. You did last year. We'll have to have some of the same things, I'm sure. The agendas look quite standard—product, policies, sales objectives, and so on.

You: Yeah, I know. We do have to cover some of the same areas each year. Maybe it's time to change the look of things, however. I did dictate the agenda for last year, but I thought since you've been given the responsibility, you might have some suggestions. (You're bringing Mary back to the objective.)

Mary: Well, one thing I'd like to see, if we could make time for it, would be to have the product presentation include some real sales technique training. The new model has so many great benefits to it. . . .

You: It does. The sales organization will love it. When you say
         we could teach sales techniques along with the initial pre-
         sentation, how would you do that? (Open question.)

Mary: You know how the advertising and sales promotion people
         always do their splashy audiovisual presentation of the ad
         campaign? Well, we could do the same sort of thing with
         product presentation. We have all those new video moni-
         tors and tape units. Why couldn't we put together a show
         with a sales rep actually presenting the new model to a
         prospect?

You: Maybe this is premature, but have you considered what
         kinds of costs that will involve? Have you or the training
         people tried it, or would we have to go outside to get it
         done? I'm interested in the idea, but you'll have to tell me
         about it. (A little challenge, but softened by subsequent in-
         terest statements that suggest areas for further response.)

Mary: We sent Marvin over to a conference on video production
         when we bought the new equipment, and he has done
         some very fine experimental work with it. In fact, he and
         Sally have put together a little segment for the training
         department—low-cost and very good quality. I'll arrange
         to have you see it. (Now Mary is coming through.)

You: I'd like to. Well, let's think about that as one of our possi-
         ble changes. Is there anything else we might do dif-
         ferently? (Keep pursuing.)

Mary: One thing I've wondered about—the territory revisions. In
         last year's meeting, the field sales manager did that from
         the platform. He explained the reasons behind the
         changes, but people weren't listening. They were too busy
         looking over the change sheets. If there were only a better
         way to do that. . . . (Mary is turning the tables on you.)

You: You didn't feel that worked too well. I admit it's usually a
         mixed-up part of the meeting, but Frank has always done
         it that way. I'll talk to him and see if he has ever given any
         thought to doing it differently. What about the presenta-

	tion you make? I thought that went very nicely last year. What's new for this year? (Open questions keep taking the topic out further.)
Mary:	You know we've been working on the new sales manual. The section on sales services is finished. If you're going to talk about the new manual, why don't we skip my presentation, make a handout of the section, and I'll make myself available to discuss it with individuals during luncheons and coffee breaks?

When the meeting with Mary ends, it ends on this note: We're going to explore the idea of developing a video presentation of the new model. A good opportunity for participative discussion has been identified for Frank, the field sales manager. An agreement is made that Mary will not make a formal presentation, and you'll include her material in your remarks. The whole flavor of the sales meeting will be different. And you can bet that Mary will be back with other suggestions. Another good bet: She'll work like crazy to make this year's meeting come off perfectly!

Now, let's take a short look at the meeting between the manager and Sam. The circumstances are different. The meeting with Mary was one of opportunity. The meeting with Sam is centered on a problem. Sam supervises your sales accounting and warranty control organization. He has about 25 people in a busy office situation. Personnel records for the past month indicate that the absentee rate is higher than normal, and you have heard complaints that there have been delays in processing paper.

You:	Sam, your department has had a lot of absenteeism in the past few weeks. My guess is that you've already looked into that. I thought we might talk about it for just a little while. Maybe you have some suggestions for turning that around.
Sam:	It *was* more than usual. Seven people accounted for 90 percent of it. What ticks me off is that five of them work in one section. I talked to the section leader about it.

You: Did she have an explanation? What did she say was the problem?

Sam: She says it's because we worked the crew overtime so many days last month. Too much overtime and they play sick.

You: That's a possibility. People seem to have the idea that they can take off after they've worked overtime. But I get the feeling that you think there's more to it than that. . . . (Essentially, an open question.)

Sam: There may be. The section leader is fairly new. A nice person, but new to that job. I've trained her and had other people work with her. The whole crew is on today and has been all week. It could be a passing thing. (Sam hopes so.)

You: Is there some way—or several ways—that we can prevent the same thing in the future? For instance, does this sort of thing occur on certain days more than others, and are there steps we can take to let people know we're not willing to put up with short attendance? (You're actually telling Sam to act.)

Sam: Well, I've been thinking about republishing that old attendance instruction we used to have. You know, the one that says people should notify the office early, schedule preplanned absences for personal reasons far in advance, and so forth. Maybe that alone would tell people we're not pleased with things as they are.

You: Might be worth a try. If you owned the company, what would you do? (That's as open as possible.)

Sam: Oh, boy, if I owned it. . . . Seriously, I've been thinking of holding a meeting with the people. (He's asking if you agree.)

You: Which people? The ones who have been absent or all of them? (The ball is back in Sam's court.)

Sam: Just the absentees, I guess. (You have helped him to decide.)

You: That might do it. What more do you intend to do about the section leader?

Sam: Well, she just came out of that same section. I promoted her
        when old Martha left. She knows the work, and she's good
        at it, but she hasn't learned to take charge. Maybe I should
        sit down with her—like this—and see if she recognizes her
        own difficulties. That might help. (The system moves
        down!)
You: A good idea. Let me know how it works out.

You really have given Sam some direction, but he walks away
thinking the course of action was his idea. Who cares? Sam will sit
down with the new section leader, and something constructive is
bound to happen. If it doesn't, you still have the power to make it
happen in different ways. And you might just have uncovered another course of action to consider. Why, indeed, did the section
have so much overtime in the first place? That's been such a standard procedure that everyone seems to accept it. Your next session
with Sam and others who are affected by it may address a different
objective.

I have gone through endless arguments with people who claim
that the consultive approach takes too much time. Say it and get it
over with! Be directive and get the job moving! Unfortunately, the
quick action results in protracted action, because the licking of
wounds consumes many hours and lasts many days. In Mary's case,
she'll throw herself into the planning of the meeting as though it
were her very own. In Sam's case, he will take action willingly that
he might otherwise have taken grudgingly.

When we give middle managers a chance, they manage themselves and others as well as we might have managed them ourselves—or better!

18

The Best Meetings Involve Leadership, Participation, and Results

If you're a typical manager, you attend staff meetings, and you hold them. If the ones you hold bear a striking resemblance to the ones you attend, that's also typical. Manager see, manager do. There is nothing wrong with following patterns—if the patterns you follow yield the results you want. Pause and consider, however, whether you are satisfied with *your own* reactions to the meetings your boss holds. Do you leave the conference room or office with fresh ideas and renewed resolve to carry your department onward and upward? Or do you leave with the thought that you're glad the session is over, so you can get back to the really important things you have to do? The final, vital, and true evaluation of any performance lies with the audience. Would your staff line up at the box office to buy tickets for your meetings?

I have attended staff meetings in which the manager sat pompously behind his desk and indulged in self-serving monologues. I have been at staff meetings where the manager conducted what appeared to be a press conference with his subordinates, and—it's true—at the end of such meetings, his No. 1 lackey stood up and said, "Thank you, Mr. Blank." The first time I saw it happen, I thought it was mere coincidence, but the second time I knew it was standard operating procedure. Then there was the national sales manager who had won acclaim running a regional sales operation and had won so many contests that the house organ dubbed him

"King of the Salesmen." His name was Richard, so he literally assumed the title "King Richard." He ordered a round table for his conference room, called his subordinates "knights," and held "court" each week. Little did he know that it was King *Arthur* whose court was known as the "Knights of the Round Table!"

Most corporate structures are geared to a pass-down of information. Staff meetings held on the top floor result in staff meetings held on down through the organization. Announcements made in the upper echelon on Monday morning get communicated at lower levels by Monday afternoon or Tuesday morning. It can be very orderly. It can be very sterile. It doesn't have to be either.

I once had a manager who held staff meetings that were interesting and open to participation by all members. My assumption was that he was simply copying a pattern of corporate meetings. Then one day he asked if I could attend his boss's staff meeting in his place. I did. What a difference! The upper-level meeting was orderly, quiet, informative—and dull. The content could simply have been typed up and distributed in the offices of staff members. A question was asked here and there, but much reserve was in evidence, because the staff member who asked a question was always answered in a manner suggesting that he or she wasn't listening or hadn't understood what had been said.

My manager would come out of that environment, return to his office, assemble his staff, and pass on the information relevant to our operation. But he encouraged discussion. He prompted questions. He reserved at least a portion of each session for the purpose of brainstorming solutions to problems. He required each of us to make a short, informal report of what was happening in our individual departments, so that our counterparts in other departments would have a big picture of our total operation. His subordinate managers leaned on one another, helped one another, and yet operated quite independently. We were a team—productive, cooperative, supportive, and still separately responsible for our own portion of the organization. That, in my opinion, is what staff meetings are all about.

Individual conferences with managers are necessary, because each member of a staff has separate and unique operating responsibilities and circumstances. A middle manager deserves some of his or her boss's time and attention away from the crowd. It's in the one-on-one that the best coaching and counseling is done, and it's in that environment that complaints and differences should be taken care of. But there are times and circumstances in which a broader application of participation is indicated. The staff meeting serves that purpose if it is conducted properly and participated in correctly. You may not be able to effect much change in your boss's staff meetings, but you surely can turn your own into idea-exchanging, work-sharing, and team-building experiences for your subordinates. Hopefully, they'll copy your pattern as they carry the word down!

For a moment, let's build a hypothetical staff. You head a division that is autonomous. Your staff includes a director for each of the following: manufacturing, engineering, sales, service, finance, and personnel. On the surface, the manufacturing people make the product, and the sales people sell it, and never the twain shall meet. But the sales people are having a problem with a certain product, so you hold a session with the sales director. He says it's manufacturing's fault. You hold a meeting with manufacturing. The manufacturing director says the product wasn't engineered properly. When you talk to the engineering guy, he says it's all caused by the fact that finance won't put money into the project. Finance says the problem lies with the workforce—see personnel. Meanwhile, the service department is working overtime to fix the product in the field, so they're asking personnel to hire people and finance to pay the bill. Have we left anyone out?

Certainly, each department has its own problems. But since all the problems interrelate, isn't there *some* reason for going beyond the individual consultation to a group process? The group may include all the staff or just segments of it. Maybe one session would include manufacturing, engineering, and finance. Perhaps another would put sales, service, and manufacturing together—not to point fingers at one another, but to attack a single problem from a variety of angles. Companies that have adopted value analysis or value control approaches to product development or internal changes find that making a creative group out of people representing different disciplines yields tremendous results. I sat in on such groups at General Electric and Chrysler and found them fascinating. At Chrysler, for instance, a group made up of an engineer, a manufacturing manager, a purchasing agent, and a finance specialist came up with a cost-cutting device that saved the corporation over a quarter of a million dollars in the first year. And none of those individuals, working on his or her own, could have come up with such an item!

Where the impact of problems and opportunities is separate, deal with individuals. Where the impact overlaps, deal with groups. And although the techniques of dealing with groups often parallel those of dealing with individuals, there are a few added factors worth our consideration. Here are a few that I believe to be the more important ones:

First, consider the group you're working with. If your staff meetings have traditionally been the information-handout sessions so common in business, you may not have considered how individuals will interface with one another in a participative session. Often, the person who is quiet in an individual conference becomes quite vocal in a group. And then there's the person who speaks right up face-to-face but clams right up in the company of his or her peers. Take inventory of the sensitivities of the components as you analyze the whole. What you discover may help you in your overall planning of meeting content and approach.

Decide on the purpose—the objective—of the meeting. You may want to have a dual purpose; begin with the routine information pass-down and then launch into the problem solving or opportunity seeking on a sharing basis. It is best to have one objective out of the way before entering into the other, because it's difficult for a group to shift gears from passive to active and then back again. Given a choice, I'd opt for getting the announcements out of the way first, then taking on the interacting portion later.

Build an agenda and timetable. For just a staff meeting? Sure, if it's important enough to hold, it's important enough to plan. A planned meeting moves along, and an unplanned one just stumbles along. Your plan can be little more than notes on a 3" × 5" card. That will do three things for you—assure that you cover every item you want to, help you do it on an orderly and timely basis, and keep you in full control of the action. There is something about a meeting leader's notes that bespeaks authority in a quiet but noticeable way.

Where possible, pick subjects that have broad interest and will draw wide involvement. Reserve the pinpointed issues for select, small groups. Also reserve the finger-pointing issues for times when only the finger-pointers are invited in. Among departmentwide topics might be budget parings, workforce adjustments, cost reductions to which everyone can contribute, policy-building recommendations, and the like. And never choose topics for group involvement that are strictly academic; if you discuss policy, for instance, be sure that the fruits of the discussion ultimately will be reported upward where policy is made. Participation should never be considered make-work or "let's pretend" activity.

If you intend to discuss a problem or opportunity on which participants may have information or opinions that could be enhanced by premeeting preparation, be sure to make an advance announcement of your intentions. "At the Monday morning staff meeting, we'll discuss budget projections in an effort to effect last-quarter savings." Any responsible manager would scour the files to be sure his or her department is properly represented and protected. Intelligent discussions are just as simple to achieve as speculative ones, and they're a lot more productive.

Most publications on how to run an effective meeting—and I have written at least three of them myself—concern themselves with the staging of larger meetings. Often they are filled with helpful hints on planning and presenting and discussion leading of a sort beyond the needs of the average staff meeting. Read such publications but don't let them frighten you. Your meetings are more intimate and less in need of tight preparations or precision handling. If, however, you'd like to know all the ins and outs of meetings, there are two publications I can recommend: Contact the National Society of Sales Training Executives (1040 Woodcock Rd., Orlando, FL 32803) and inquire about Jim Rapp's booklet on getting participation in meetings. Or get in touch with *Sales & Marketing Management Magazine* (633 Third Ave., New York, NY 10017) for a booklet written by Homer Smith on how to conduct all kinds of meetings. For our purposes at this time, just these few suggestions:

If your staff meeting is being held merely to provide members with information, pull the group together in your office. When you pass down policy or news that requires only modest clarification and discussion, your being behind your desk in the control position is quite acceptable. But if you hope to spend a major portion of time in a participative mode, move to the conference room or to a conference table in your own office. You are no less in control, but you make the participants more amenable to jumping in with both feet. The same phenomenon occurs when the conference leader stands or sits: Standing sets up a psychological barrier and focuses attention on the leader; sitting breaks down the barrier and spreads attention among the participants.

Learn how to cope with "types." They are variously described as "the silent type," "the talker," "the know-it-all," "the arguer," "the stubborn soul," "the rambler," "the griper," "the distracter," "the misunderstander," "the antagonist," and "the apple polisher." Just those terms help you identify them, and you very likely have some of them on your own staff. Managers who manage managers must learn to step in and stimulate the noncontributor, cool down the hothead, and quiet the bigmouth. There are ways of doing it, but before we explore them, we'll take a look at a few other classifications that will be familiar.

Do you have someone attending your group meetings whom you

might label "the expert"? This is the person who is full of facts, bowls you over, tries to quick-close you and the others to his or her point of view, doesn't hesitate to leave the impression that not following such a point of view is sheer folly. Annoying as such an individual may be, he or she generally comes armed with detail, has assurance born of prior thought and experience, and possesses conviction that is worth harnessing. You give such a contributor an opportunity to make points, but you also treat those points as only one side of the debate. When confronted by "an expert," listen carefully and also plot a means of getting balanced contributions from others.

How about "the politician"? This is the person who name-drops, gathers votes, involves other participants in such a way that they find opposing difficult. This individual is more concerned about support than substance and wants to win more than to solve problems. Listen to and acknowledge the contributions of "the politician" and don't forget that if his or her support is real, your project may succeed as a result of it. "Politicians" are circumspect individuals who line up with winners, so make it clear to such a person that the discussion aims not at a popular vote, but at a workable solution. You don't get on the *politician's* side—get him or her on *yours.*

Then there's "the country boy." Country boys begin by saying they don't know much about the issue, but it just seems as if. . . . They're the ones who can throw themselves at your feet and then stomp you to death at the same time. Part of the act is to build a hedge against possible error, but sometimes their counsel is worth listening to. Such people are generally open to ideas, so don't dismiss their contributions. Let them play a part in the balancing and peer disciplining of "the expert" and "the politician." "The country boy" will drive them crazy and keep them in line.

You may have a staff member who could carry the title of "the sandbagger." One of these is enough in any group. This type sits out the early stages, holds back information, waits for others to make mistakes, trumps aces, and concludes by saying, "If you had asked me, I would have told you." Don't despair: "The sandbagger" has a sense of timing that may be valuable. You can count on such an individual to wait until the problem is defined and enough data produced before coming up with solutions. Balance this person against the others, and the results will be fine. If you can get his or her involvement earlier, the conclusion will be reached sooner.

If you have a staff member who could be called "the hitchhiker," you can learn from him or her, too. "The hitchhiker" doesn't originate, plays the scavenger, uses discards advantageously, puts three other people's ideas into a composite, and stakes a claim on it as an original idea. Managers who employ such individuals to good advantage recognize that by using ideas or idea fragments it's possible to create better ideas, and good ideas become great ones. "Hitchhiker" ideas work best for the group and less well for the individual if they are encouraged earlier and more often. That minimizes the trump playing and makes a better team effort of the discussion.

Finally, we have "the wet puppy." This is the person who sulks if it doesn't go his or her way. If the project isn't carried out in accordance with his or her own suggestions, it simply won't work at all. Or this is the type that says, "Your ideas may sound fine, but I'll end up doing all the work to make the thing succeed." You can't be too impressed by such complaining, but neither can you ignore "the wet puppy." He or she tends to be a realist and looks down the road for potholes and roadblocks. They may, indeed, be there. You'll find, however, that others in the group will hop in and either minimize the difficulties or offer to help overcome them.

Look for these types. The extent to which they can help or hurt the participative effort is directly related to the way they are managed in a meeting. A few simple handling techniques will improve your chances of getting positive reactions rather than suffering negative ones. Here they are:

• Get the group into the habit of recognizing that they are *contributors* to a decision, not the decision makers. This minimizes the efforts of individual participants to win cases. If they do win points, that's fine, but the emphasis is no longer on winner-take-all.

- If ideas presented are good and appear to have mutual approval, don't hesitate to say, "That's what we'll do." Your subordinates expect you to make decisions and are pleased to see that you can make them on the spot.

- If ideas seem to have a variety of plus and minus characteristics, or if the solution isn't quite clear in your own mind, don't hesitate to say, "I appreciate the good thinking you've put into this, and I'll be back for more ideas or will make a decision later." Your subordinates would rather see you postpone a decision in such cases than make a bad one.

- When you have a variety of characters such as was described earlier, your simplest protection is to maintain balance in the contributions. Shift the spotlight from the dominating personalities to the quieter ones from time to time. Draw out the noncontributors early. Given an opportunity, the "experts" and the "politicians" will always be first and strongest in their offerings, and the "country boys," "sandbaggers," and "hitchhikers" will always be slowest to contribute. Pass the action around. By doing so, you'll minimize conflict and jealousy.

- Keep the discussion on track. If it wanders, pull it back. Don't hesitate to say, "Although that's an important thing to consider, Sylvia, let's hold it for a little later." Then be sure you do go back to Sylvia's concern when the time is right.

- Be careful of put-downs. Don't attack participants. If you do, you can be sure they'll be nonparticipants the next time around. Difficult people should be handled in private consultation sessions.

- If issues seem to be clear-cut enough to make decisions on, and you do make the decisions on the spot, the meeting may also be the place to make the assignments. If your operation is properly organized, work-related assignments should be automatic. If, however, the assignment doesn't fall neatly into a subordinate's normal area of responsibility, you might ask for volunteers, or you could team up a pair of enthusiasts. Or if there are two who have divergent views, you could pair them up to work out a plan that meets their—and your—overall approval. To be put on one's own is the middle manager's idea of heaven!

• Stay in control. That doesn't mean the control of minds, but the control of behavior. Your strengths as a manager will be revealed more in this than in any other managerial act you perform. Letting people in takes more courage than keeping people out. Getting people to work together takes more skill than playing the lone hand.

Meetings take time. That time is wasted if you assemble the wrong people on the wrong issues, but it's well spent if you get the right people concentrating on matters that are important to the company—and to them. Meetings take work. So does everything else a manager does. The work is wasted if meetings are poorly planned and handled and if the net result is negligible. If your immediate subordinate staff numbers five or six people—the norm in most organizations—your *one-hour* meeting takes up five or six hours of valuable management time and effort . . . not including your own. If your managers or supervisors walk away from your meeting feeling that they have been heard, have made a contribution to corporate thinking through you, have had a chance to clarify their own position and problems, know more about their roles in the organization, see goals more clearly, and can identify with those goals, you couldn't have spent their time better.

And you? You'll get more insight regarding the capabilities and the attitudes of your subordinates as a result of seeing them interface with one another. You'll be able to make midcourse corrections better and performance appraisals more accurately. Your decisions will be both more productive and more popular. What better way could you spend your time?

19

When You Prove You Can Stand
On Your Own Two Feet,
I'll Get Off Your Back!

One reason managers hesitate to delegate fully or to allow much input from below is their concern about the ability of their subordinates to make correct judgments and take appropriate actions on their own. That's a valid reason, for after all, a manager is judged by both the productivity and the absence of difficulties generated in his or her department. If you're going to get the blame for whatever goes wrong, why risk anything by letting someone else get too involved? The answer to that concern is basic: If you can get subordinates to see that you have a workable system for analyzing situations, defining problems, coming up with suitable courses of action, *and get them to work by that same system,* a major part of your worries should be over.

Working by your system may not mean that subordinates will produce conclusions that are identical to yours; two people faced with the same set of data may still perceive facts in different lights and relationships. But operating by a similar system of problem solving and decision making *will* produce:

- An assurance that a step-by-step approach will be taken which minimizes overlooking facts and possible angles.
- A uniformity of approach that allows you and others to participate at any juncture where outside help is needed.

○ A decision that, while it may not match your expectations, will not be so far off the mark that total failure will result.

In short, by taking a systematic approach and teaching your subordinates to do the same, you are making it possible for them to do things their way—*your* way. The system becomes a built-in supervision factor that keeps you from having to be the ever present watcher and corrector. If, as we contended earlier, middle managers resent close supervision, your teaching them to stand on their own two feet will let them know you're ready to get off their backs.

Some of the best problem solvers and decision makers I have ever known would have real difficulty in telling others just how to go about it. Many would say, "You simply take all the facts into consideration and decide which action would do you the most good and the least harm." Others would contend that they just used "plain common sense." Neither of these approaches makes for a teachable routine. Good sense wasn't parceled out in equal portions to all of us, and I have the feeling that intuition is less a matter of special gift than it is a matter of repeated and rehearsed application of both the deductive and inductive processes. What worked before will probably work again.

Not to demean business decision making, but to put it in true perspective, it would be fair to say that some decisions could be made by flipping a coin. Heads, we go and tails, we stay. Heads, we buy and tails, we don't. Look at all the judgment and hard thinking that went into the creating of the Edsel. It should have been a success. If someone had offered me a franchise for selling hula hoops, I wonder whether I would have taken it on. I thought they were dumb, but millions of people bought them.

Most business decisions are reversible. If you decide at first not to try something, you can always decide later to do it. If you decide to do something, you can quit if it doesn't work out. Obviously, you can't do that with all decisions: The business landscape is littered with the debris of bad guesses, poor hunches, and unlucky coin tosses. If possible, we'd like something better in the way of decision making and problem solving. If nothing else, a systematic approach can keep us from making the same blunder twice.

We are in a computer age. Data processing and data communications are so refined and so attainable that they're widely used. We can use electronics to collect, assemble, compute, and compare information, but we still have to know what information to call for before the systems will do us any good. That means we still have to make human judgments regarding the nature of any given situation, identify the problem or problems that underlie that situation, and be circumspect enough to understand what the data yield is telling us. Although our new automation may replace workers on the assembly line and clerical staff in the bullpen, the future remains very promising for managers who can think and decide.

Here is a step-by-step problem-solving routine you can teach your subordinates. Chances are it matches almost completely with what you now do in reaching your own decisions. Admittedly, it's short and lacks the sophistication of many of the more popular and complex techniques abroad today. They may be better, because they delve more deeply into the subject; but I am suspicious of some approaches, because they are so procedural that people get caught up in the process and forget what problem they're trying to solve. Also, you'll note that I use the terms "problem solving" and "decision making" interchangeably. I see them as one and the same: We make decisions to solve problems.

1. Begin by identifying the situation that currently exists. Here we'll get fussy, for a good reason. The situation is a condition behind which problems lie. Example: Sales are down. That is a fact, a condition. *Why* sales are down is the question and the problem. The situation is the effect, and the problem is the cause. I make that distinction so that we forestall quick conclusions like this: "Sales are down, Mike. You had better get out into the field and get the sales force cracking. We can't go on like this." Poor Mike. He is sent on a mission with directions to solve a problem that may not even exist. If more time was spent in the initial stage of separating

cause from effect, we would do better problem solving, and we would have fewer unhappy middle managers.

So we look at the situation. We ask ourselves:

o What's happening now?
o Am I pleased with what's happening?
o Is it meeting earlier objectives?
o What are we losing or failing to gain as a result of what we're now doing?

What we may discover is that we are quite pleased with the results, and that no problem exists. Or (and this is important) we may discover that there is room for improvement—not a real problem, but an opportunity to do something better. A good example of this is in marketing. Sales volume, unit and dollar yields, may be quite acceptable, but there could be one item in the line that's disappointing. Perhaps a little extra effort would change that situation. Is there something we could be doing here at headquarters or something they could be doing out in the field that would improve the situation? Some problems are severe, some are minor, but good managers don't overlook any of them. Successful companies are those in which minor adjustments are being made all the time. Losers are the ones that don't notice until it's too late.

2. Once we discover that the situation is not to our liking, we go looking for the problem—the cause. Two sensible questions have to be asked:

o What's being done, or not being done, that creates such a situation?
o Is there more than one cause?

Using the sales example given earlier, it might be wise to go to the charts to see whether sales are down in all sales regions or districts, or down in certain products and not in others. Could it be that sales are not materializing because the factory isn't producing the needed items in sufficient volume? Has a competitor cut prices or introduced a new model? By asking many questions and by poking into many corners, we get a picture of what needs to be fixed. Surprisingly, many managers don't do this step carefully enough and rely on hunches or prejudices. When a subordinate is sent out to "get the sales reps cracking," and the problem is competitive pricing, poor delivery from the factory, or poor quality, it's little wonder that the subordinate feels he or she is being poorly managed.

3. At this point, problem evaluation is in order. So we ask questions like these:

- Is it really a problem?
- How big a problem is it?
- Is it the *only* problem?
- Is it the *real* problem?
- Is it worth solving?

Sales are down. They're down in two districts. In one district, three of the six sales reps quit last month, went to work for competitors. Replacement reps are now being trained as quickly as they can be hired.

Is there a problem? Is it worth solving? You'd better believe it! You're already ahead of me on this: What kind of manager do we have in that market? Would it pay us to take a closer look at how the district is being run? You see, when the problem is evaluated carefully, it's likely to lead us down trails we might not have thought of exploring before.

In the second district, we discover that the town's major industry was shut down, thousands of people are unemployed, and not much of anything is selling there. A problem? Yes, but chances are we can't do much more about that one than wait and make plans to study and revise the operation accordingly.

4. As we probe into the nature of the problem, it's normal for us to jot down some potential solutions. The important thing is not to stop at a single solution. Here, in fact, is one of those grand areas of staff involvement—the solution-generating process, which we

know could be enhanced by the variety of experiences and points of view of a well-balanced staff. We ask ourselves questions like:

○ Is more than one solution possible?
○ Does one solution create another problem?
○ Which solution is simpler or less expensive than others?
○ If we apply this or that solution, will it solve all or most of the problems?

Managers often do wrong things for right reasons and right things for wrong reasons. By pausing to mull over the available solutions, we can forestall many mistakes. Often, when the problem is examined and the potential solutions are studied, we come up with more than one solution. This allows us to attack the problem from several sides. For instance, there may be a short-range and a long-range solution. If we apply both, we rid ourselves of the current annoyance, and we also guard against recurrence. Many economists contended during the 1980–81 economic malaise that the seeds of failure were sown years ago by managers who did quick fixes to boost single-year profitability at the expense of long-range stability. The automotive industry was a prime example.

5. We choose a solution. The analysis gives us good answers to the following questions:

○ Is there a *best* solution, and can we use it?
○ If we choose it, what steps must be taken?
○ Are the resources available to implement it?
○ Who does it?

Here again, we have potential for interesting and worthwhile staff involvement. Out of this step comes the action plan and the action. That brings us quickly to the final steps. . . .

6. The solution—action taken to bring about change—and. . . .

7. A new situation. If problem solving is to be worth anything, we should always look at the new situation to assure ourselves that what we did to change the previous situation has been effective. And the new situation deserves a careful monitoring for an ex-

tended period of time to be sure the solution continues to work. Even more interesting is the possibility that in examining the new situation, we may discover other problems or new opportunities. Or we may conclude that one of the solutions we chose not to apply earlier deserves application now.

Good management decisions aim at being perfect and permanent, but good management decision makers recognize that it's never safe to walk away from yesterday's solutions without taking a look at tomorrow's potential problems.

In sequence, then, problem solving looks like this:

- Examining the situation—is it satisfactory?
- Defining the problem—what lies behind the unsatisfactory situation?
- Evaluating the problem—how big, how real is it?
- Analyzing the solutions—how many ways are there to fix it, and will they work?
- Planning the solution—what steps, what resources, who does it?
- Solving the problem—taking corrective action.
- Examining the situation—is it satisfactory, better than before?

The example set by the manager is the practice that will be adopted by the subordinate. The opportunity for both leadership and involvement is everywhere present in the problem-solving/decision-making process. The best managers give ongoing demonstrations of their own approach to handling problems and taking suitable action. They also groom subordinates to be able to take on problem solving individually and in groups. You have managers and supervisors reporting to you who will gladly absorb the workload if only they know they are being credited with the talent and the judgment needed to take the job from problem to solution.

This is the key to effective managing of managers—allowing them to get in *early* on problems, giving them a chance to *do* the thinking or *contribute* to the thinking required to develop suitable solutions, and then turning the job over to them for handling. All too often, the process is already at midstream before the subordinate is asked to get in on it. Then it's a case of task assumption—the very thing subordinates resent most.

Observe these three managerial statements. Which would you most appreciate if the speaker were your boss?

- "Jim, there's a tie-up out in the shipping room. I've received numerous complaints about late arrivals on much-needed orders. Go out there, get hold of your foremen, and tell them we can't put up with that. Have them watch out for priority orders, handle those quickly, and if necessary, ship them a faster way. You might want to hire some part-time help at the end of the day to make sure those orders get out. Let me know what happens."

- "Jim, I've received a number of complaints from customers about late arrivals on much-needed orders. Would you check into that and let me know what needs to be done about it?"

- "Jim, I've received a number of complaints from customers about late arrivals on much-needed orders. Can you turn that situation around?"

Three degrees of direction. The first manager had it all figured out. The second manager asked to be helped or offered to help in the decision making. The third just cut the subordinate loose. Either of the last two instructions would be more pleasing to the subordinate than the first. Either of the last two would also get the job done faster and better, and the results of the fix would last much longer.

If subordinate managers don't like to solve problems, they don't belong in management. If upper-level managers solve all the problems by themselves, they don't need subordinate managers—just lots of workers. When managers get other managers working on their own, everybody profits.

20

Moving Targets Are Hard to Hit, But They Give You An Excuse When You Miss!

We covered the advantages of involving managers in goal setting in an earlier chapter. If you do so, your success will be achieved in direct proportion to your subordinates' ability to handle goal-setting assignments. Just as you coached them on problem solving and decision making, you'll want to give them some help in goal setting.

You have your own goals. Maybe you didn't have any say in what those goals were. Quotas get dumped on managers, and managers dump quotas on supervisors, and so it goes. You don't want to perpetuate that error, so you involve your subordinates in setting their own goals in such a way that your goals are reached. The following is an oversimplified look at what your approach will be.

Establish a system of forward planning. Whatever your corporate year is, match it with a plan. Launch the program on a wide-open basis—"From your own departmental point of view, what would you like to accomplish in the coming year?" Include in that very general invitation the instruction that current programs and ongoing responsibilities belong in that projection just as new opportunities do. Be frank in saying that what goes into the forward plan will be discussed with each manager and that ultimately it may become part of firmly set objectives. Be equally frank in admitting that some of the items may have to be postponed. But underscore the thought that if an idea isn't in the forward plan, it won't be discussed, considered, or included.

When forward plans are in the formative stage, they deserve to be general. That not only makes the first pass at them simpler, faster, and more noncommittal, but it allows for creative input by you and the managers who write them. You'll discover, however, that some managers are perfectly willing to prepare polished drafts for your examination and are equally willing to redraft them for approval. Never discourage that kind of initiative but don't demand it. Some of the best managers are not given to laborious writing, and that shouldn't defeat the concept of forward planning. Since you are going to work each of the plans over on an individual basis in conference with your subordinates, no two plans have to be alike.

At the conclusion of your preliminary discussion of the forward plan, provide each manager with a suggested format. Probably you'll prefer that each item be listed separately, with brief notations on specifics included below. Request that at the end of each item a projected volume of achievement and a target date be included. Ask for two copies, so that you can hold one and the subordinate can hold the other during your discussion. As the plan gets tighter, the discussion gets more exacting, and the commitment grows stronger. Let it be understood that the initial submission may not be the final submission. You'll work on the refinement together at your next session.

The advantage of taking forward plans through rough drafts in the early stages is that you can remind your subordinates of omissions and can prompt additions that seem reasonable and worthwhile. That may not stop with the first time around; in the intervening days between first and second counseling sessions, both parties may have further thoughts. It's also possible that conditions may change as the forward plan is being developed. You'll want to account for that and for the inclusion of requests coming down to you from upstairs.

Let's follow the progress of a single item on a forward plan from first draft to final draft:

• *First draft:* Improve quality, with special attention to Models C, G, and M.

(You ask questions about what kind of quality improvements the manager has in mind, to what extent that quality has to be improved, and how he or she might intend to do it.)

• *Second draft:* Improve quality of finished product, with emphasis on Models C, G, M, and W. Specific attention will be given to coatings, hardware application, and stress tests. Improvement measurements will include 10 percent lower end-of-line rejection and 10 percent reduction in warranty claims. The project will require training and may include a contest.

(Your consultation has added one item to the list, pointed out areas selected for improvement, established specific goals, and named methods by which the goals can be reached. You ask in the second conference when the training will be completed, when the contest will be held, and when the first improvements are expected to occur.)

• *Final draft* (the following items are added to the second draft): The project will require training, which is scheduled to begin by March 1 and be completed by March 15. If immediate improvements do not reflect a 5 percent lower end-of-line rejection rate, a contest will be introduced for the entire month of April. Full achievement of rejection and claim reductions is targeted for May 30 and should be maintained or improved through the balance of the year.

What you have accomplished in the foregoing exercise is the setting of the target. Some managers don't want targets that are stable. If they can make them loose, then who can blame them if they miss? "If I *said* I'd get it done sometime this year, don't trouble me about it until midway through December. You know I'll get around to it."

That doesn't work. Get fixed targets and show progress regularly. That does work. I learned that many years ago when I taught school. My students had ten assignments they were required to complete in the final four weeks of the semester. In my first experience with the program, I made specific assignments on a daily basis. Then I decided to try making adults of teenagers by laying out the whole program, putting the chart of completed assignments on the wall, and letting nature take its course.

The first week was worrisome. Only the eager beavers took on the challenge. The second week, we had significant improvement. Then it began to happen. The visual reminder of things not done was a great motivator. The third week was packed with activity, as was the fourth. But what was significant about the fourth week was the fact that some students came up and asked if they could redo certain assignments in order to improve their grades. Why not? They did more and they did better, and I handed out higher grades that semester than ever before. The young men and women in that group had an objective and a timetable, and they proved themselves capable of rising to the task. (Or should I have said goal?)

The more specific the goal and the more evident the progress, the greater the motivation. Test that in the business world, and it will prove its validity.

Counseling develops greater understanding, acceptance, and commitment. The manager who goes through these steps with subordinates will discover that the objectives set by the subordinate will, in most cases, be more demanding than if they were set by the manager. Care should be taken in this regard, also, to be sure that the goals set meet the following standards:

• They should be measurable. If they can't be measured in volume, they can be measured in percent of improvement. If they can't be quantified, they can at least be dated—in operation by a certain date, effective, productive, or completed by a certain date. In this regard, managers should get their subordinate managers or supervisors to present goals in terms of the subordinates' own measurements. For instance, a sales director may have to meet a share-of-market goal, but his or her field sales managers will have to set their goals in terms of units.

• Goals should be challenging. If last year's results were good, next year's should be better. Again, don't just accept "improved sales" as a goal, but specify units or percent of improvement. In this instance, it's important that the individual who has to meet a goal understand exactly what he or she has been able to accomplish before. If you don't know where you've been, it's hard to get excited about where you're going.

• Goals should be achievable. The impossible dream doesn't belong on the middle manager's goal list unless he or she understands that defeat is more likely than success. Good managers counsel subordinates away from the impossible—not by ridicule, but by reality.

• Goals should be accompanied by a sense of reward or penalty. The penalty may be nothing more than the knowledge that the goal wasn't met and explanations have to be made. The reward may be nothing more than a sense of accomplishment. Nobody fools anybody, however: Managers who meet objectives are managers who get good ratings and promotions. They don't have to be promised anything if they know the system is working right and that their boss knows the system.

I have worked in and around sales organizations where goals or quotas were set poorly—from above. A corporate objective is set, and this is followed by a parceling out of regional and district sales objectives. What starts as 100 ends up on the quota sheets as something like 125, because at each level the goal is bumped a little "just as insurance." Sam Salesman goes out and meets 90 percent of his objective, which is 5 percent better than his boss expected, so Sam gets a medal. What happens, of course, is that Sam will be forever convinced that doing the job 90 percent is terrific. Goals of that sort are misleading.

Goals are easy to quantify if they're production-line unit counts or sales-dollar volume. They're not so easy to put numbers on if they fall in service and support areas. But they can be set, and they can be met. And don't overlook the non-bottom-line items. If each department could cut such factors as waste, absenteeism, accidents, lost accounts, customer complaints, and the like, companies would have more interesting bottom lines.

When your individual conferences have been held, and you are satisfied with each manager's forward plan, get the staff together to let each tell the others what's going to happen. Too often people work in the dark and alone on the fulfillment of their goals. In nearly every case in which I have participated or observed, when the group process works effectively, greater cooperation results. You'll hear peers congratulate one another, like, "That's a great idea, Jan. That'll help me do. . . ." Or, "If you do that, Bill, I really won't have to do this, will I? Tell you what, you handle that part of it, and I'll pick up the other." Interaction is one of the best things that can happen to a work group.

Plans made and goals set take you only part of the way. The monitoring of the activity and accomplishment follows. Every goal should have interim goals and timetables attached to it. You should know them, and your managers should know them. And you should keep track of where people are along the way. Not doing so renders the earlier efforts worthless. A friend of mine once turned down a social engagement with me, explaining that he had to turn in his forward plan and annual objectives the following day. Then he added, "I don't know why. I never hear about them after they're in. They're either that good, or they never get looked at. I don't *dare* discover which." I knew what he meant, because I once worked in an organization that operated in that fashion. Lots of paper, but that was about all.

When goals are achieved, they should get recognition. Again, this is a great subject for staff meetings. "You've all noticed that we set a new record for shipments last month. That was one of Phil's goals for the year—to have at least one month at that level. Do you suppose we'll have another before the year is over, Phil?" Don't be surprised if Phil comes back with, "I'm going to try to make next month's even bigger." Goals achieved and rewarded tend to result in new goals that bring about new achievements.

The initiation of a goal-setting procedure is always the most difficult phase to accomplish. Managers who are unaccustomed to managing their own affairs may take to the activity with fear and suspicion. They may need support in the process, and they'll certainly need coaching and counseling. Focus attention on the substance of the forward plan and the goal, and let the form develop later. To be supercritical of composition and word selection in the introduction of a system that requires a freewheeling operator to sit down and write things out merely invites resistance. Get cooperation and interest first, then get perfection later on. Subsequent tries will show steady improvement.

If you introduce forward planning in your own organization, and it isn't something you have to do for your boss, why not make a composite of the several plans submitted to you and pass one on upstairs? The reactions will range from, "What's this?" to, "Well, that's a good idea." In the following chapter, we'll consider some of the things you might do to introduce your own ideas upward. As you read these techniques, you may also want to teach your own subordinates how they can offer suggestions to you.

21

Participation Is a Two-Way Street

When we talk about participation and the flow of ideas upward in a business organization, we seem always to put the monkey on the manager's back. "Let your people contribute to your organization's planning and decision making," we say. I've had managers respond to that with, "I'd be glad to do it, but they don't want to." Or the opposite: "I've got people on my staff who would drive you right up the wall with their attitudes about how things should be done. I can't stand the person who pushes too hard or the individual who comes in with some half-baked idea and wastes my time with it."

Then let's put the onus on the subordinate for just a moment. That, of course, means *you*, with your suggestions and advice to *your* boss. It also offers another skill you can teach those who report to you. Knowing *how* to make suggestions is not only a skill but a responsibility of any subordinate in any organization. A good idea badly presented is really no better than a poor idea, because value depends heavily on how well a concept is understood and the emotional climate in which it is received. Look at what happened to Galileo. He had a great idea but was so outspoken and indiscreet that he not only was repudiated but was taken captive by the Inquisitors and escaped torture only when he retracted his statements.

When a manager makes a suggestion downward, the idea presented is enhanced by the stamp of authority; unless it's a wholly bad idea, it's likely to be followed without much question. The idea that flows upward, on the other hand, comes from a platform of relative weakness. It's easy to see why the up-flow idea has to be sound in its concept and appropriate in its expression. It's the old saw repeated: First, find a good product, then sell it for all it's worth!

Style and substance. Let's look first at substance, because if the substance isn't right, there's little sense in applying style to it. Often subordinates don't consider that; they get a glimmer of an idea that has some attractive elements, and they run to their manager and start to explain it. The insufficient homework they've done begins to show immediately, because they haven't connected all the dots, and the picture doesn't take shape. Their enthusiasm is overwhelming, but their knowledge is underwhelming. Halfway through the explanation, the boss raises a question. The subordinate is either embarrassed or annoyed that the great idea is being challenged. That adds emotional fuel to the fire. The reaction is either one of personal rejection or the feeling that the boss doesn't care to hear good ideas. It takes us a long time to realize that we were at fault for not having prethought the proposal properly.

Seldom are business problems so time-intensive that an extra hour or an extra day can't be spent on refining suggestions. Remember what we discussed earlier, in the chapter on problem solving? One item dealt with whether the solution of this problem would cause other problems. That's a common factor in ideas that get turned down—the second wave of problems. I recall a cartoon caption—a sketch of a meeting, with charts on display and the manager saying, "I'm going to save money for this company if it takes our last nickel!" There was once an agency account executive who used to try to sell me training materials by saying, "Just think, you can train 1,000 salesmen with this, and they'll each sell two or three extra units!" That was fine, except that they would have had to sell *ten* extra units each in order to pay the bill for training them the way he proposed to do it. A little more thought might have brought that suggestion into line, in terms of either costs or achievement.

Prethinking a proposal doesn't have to be laborious. It doesn't have to be formal. It does require thinking through the steps required to make the idea work and the possible hazards in applying it. What you get when you spend a little time in advance is:

○ An idea that shows potential for working.
○ A presentation that's organized and understandable.
○ Ammunition to fend off counterattacks made on the idea.
○ A running start on implementing the program if it's approved.

The best proposals I've had presented to me were those made by thoughtful subordinates who had done the kind of homework that revealed during the presentation that the idea had:

○ A worthwhile objective in mind.
○ Benefits that outweighed any disadvantages of cost or effort.
○ A rough plan concerning how long the project would take, what resources would be required to implement it, who would do it, and how soon results would begin to appear.
○ Available data on whether or not such an idea had ever been tried, whether it worked, and what the results were.

Many middle managers who complain that their bosses don't listen to them might take these thoughts into consideration. It might not be the boss who is at fault. I never buy a product unless I feel it will do what I want it to do, hold up under normal use, not obsolete itself overnight, or cost me more than I can afford to pay for it. Should I expect any less of an idea proposed for my business use? Managers should always think of their ideas in the light of selling techniques: Would *you* buy if you were on the other side of the table?

Managers sometimes don't buy even the very good ideas. Some of the reasons—or excuses, if you like—are these:

○ They're upstaged; they should have thought of it themselves.
○ Ideas from below are threatening. What will come up next?

- An idea something like it has been tried before, and it didn't work. (*I* did it and failed.)
- If upper management approval is required, the program would be hard to sell. Let's not stir the waters.
- If the idea is approved, the subordinate will not accept victory gracefully. Some people don't know their place.

It's unfortunate that some managers have so little self-confidence that they can't share credit with others—or so little vision that they can't see that new circumstances may make an idea that failed before work now. The whole business of a manager is to improve corporate profitability through the application of good ideas—yours or your subordinates'.

One manager confided in me that he hesitated to offer his boss an idea because the response would generally be, "Well, I don't think that will work, but we'll keep it in mind." Then, my resource went on to say, "The blankety-blank would sit on it for six months, run it upstairs, and sell it as his own. From here on in, I'm going to hold back the ideas until he gets promoted, fired, or retires. Then I'll get the job and turn the situation around." That sort of thing happens more often than we would like to believe.

That last case indicated substance that was acceptable but raises the question of style. How were those suggestions made? What personality difficulties were present? Whose fault was it? Could the same idea have been presented, accepted, and passed up through the hierarchy with the subordinate's name attached? There are many ways in which an idea can be framed for positive credit and good results.

Many managers prefer a direct approach. I have an idea, come to you, and say, "Carl, we need to do something about this, and here's how I propose doing it." That's quick, straightforward, and may be effective if the following conditions prevail:

- The subordinate has a reputation for good judgment and appropriate action.

○ The explanation is complete and to the point.
○ The suggestion bears no hint that the subordinate is either putting down the boss or grabbing glory.
○ The boss is interested in getting results and doesn't care who gets the credit for it.

Then there's the indirect approach. I have an idea and say to you, "Carl, you've probably already considered doing something about this. If you haven't come up with a plan yet, here's one thing I believe will work." That gives the boss some credit for understanding the problem and having thought about it. It will work if:

○ The subordinate knows what he or she is doing.
○ The explanation is made well and seems aimed at a true solution of the problem—regardless of who gets the credit.
○ The suggestion seems to invite discussion, not just approval.

Another approach would be the advice-seeking technique. I have an idea and say to you, "Carl, you know we've been having some problems with this. I have an idea, but I need your advice on how to go about it. How would it be if we . . . ?" This approach will work well if:

○ There's no hint of conning the boss by playing coy.
○ The subordinate's intention is to take the advice that's solicited.
○ The expectation is that the ultimate course of action may be a blend of ideas properly employed.

Argue that last approach as manipulative, if you will. It can be. It can also be an honest application of the concept that two heads are better than one. Seeking the boss's counsel, even when you believe you have most of the solution already in hand, isn't such a bad idea. Your boss got where he or she is because of knowledge, experience, and the ability to pursue opportunity—not a bad background for your source of advice.

Then there is the conditions-have-changed approach. I have an idea, but it's one that has been tried before, didn't work as well as we wanted it to, and a barrier of prejudice has been built against it in the boss's mind. I say to you, "Carl, remember when we tried this and it didn't work? Well, some of the reasons it didn't were . . . and now those things have changed. For instance. . . ." The advantage to this approach is that it speaks up early about the past deficiencies. It will work if:

- The problem you want to solve really needs solving.
- Conditions really have changed.
- There is every reason to believe that different conditions, new technology, improved capability of the workforce, and so on are such that old negatives cease to apply.
- The suggestion is given in such a way as to remove any hint of vested interest or stubborn clinging to a worn-out point of view.

Finally, there's the approach that gives credit and promises support to the person to whom the suggestion is offered. I say to you, "Carl, you mentioned that . . . and I've been thinking. . . ." In other words, the boss gets credit for the idea, and you support him or her with additional input. "Taking your idea of doing that further, how about . . . ?" One idea has grown out of another. It happens all the time. Often subordinates fail to give their manager any credit at all, and when that happens, the proposal falls on deaf ears.

Another thought on giving advice upward. Some managers and supervisors are so committed to the idea of winning every round that they lose the bout. "He who fights and runs away lives to fight another day" isn't such bad counsel in corporate life. That doesn't mean giving up or giving in; it means biding time. I recall one of my early encounters as a young supervisor working under a very resolute manager. He was so often right that I seldom took his turndowns as anything more than a condition of learning. Yet, on one occasion, I made a suggestion he rejected out-of-hand. I attempted to justify my point of view, and he finally cut me off with,

"I understand what you want done, but I don't approve of it. Unless your proposal comes back again *without those things I object to most*, I simply will not consider it."

I said, "O.K. That's that. I won't bring it up again." I started to leave his office.

I had my hand on the doorknob, when he said, "You think I'm wrong, don't you?"

"We have different points of view. But you've explained your position, and I accept it." I thanked him for his time and left.

The next day, he called me and said, "I've been thinking about our conversation of yesterday. If you have a few minutes, come down and we'll talk about it again."

We talked about it. He had given it further consideration, and although what we finally decided to do was a compromise on both parts, the project was instituted. It succeeded, and I admit the success was partly due to the fact that it wasn't done entirely my way. I never heard about that from him, however. What I did hear was, "I'm glad we went on with the project. I was opposed to it at first, but I gave it some thought, and there were good things in it. If you had argued with me, I probably would have rejected it and never given it another thought. You won my approval by demonstrating patience."

That's the word—"patience." Those of us who make suggestions upward forget that the person to whom we are making the suggestion is hearing a new idea for the first time. We, on the other hand, have thought about it and grown to love the idea. It sometimes takes time for the other person to get on track with innovation and see its value.

It would do most managers a lot of good to take a course in salesmanship. I don't recommend the high-pressure, bowl-'em-over school of selling—just the customer-oriented school. There are several basic things every sales rep has to know:

o Every presentation has to be made with the buyer's interests in mind.

- You build value in the mind of the buyer by presenting the idea in terms of its *benefits to the buyer.*
- You ask questions more than you talk. Involvement of the buyer is vital to the ultimate buying decision.
- You *let* the buyer buy.
- If you don't close on the first try, leave the door open to make a second stab at it. That's patience.

Two behaviors are worth teaching to any manager. To the subordinate, I would teach the absolute necessity of preparation, clarity of presentation, and willingness to keep an open mind to refinements based on the manager's insights and interests. To the superior, I would teach the need for careful listening and a willingness to pursue new ideas until they have proved either worth or lack of it. Without *both* those behaviors, simultaneously applied, ideas have difficulty flowing in either direction.

If your subordinates aren't feeding you worthwhile ideas, maybe you need to teach them how to do it. If your own ideas aren't selling well upstairs, you could try some of the suggestions presented here. Style *and* substance, and all parties working at them, are what make open management work.

22

Management:
Inexact Science, Unrefined Art

Show me your license to manage, and I'll show you mine. There's a Mexican standoff. We're in a profession that isn't one, plying a science that thus far hasn't been defined, and pursuing an art for which standards haven't been set. Each school of business establishes its own curriculum, and few of them match program-for-program. On the hiring line, each corporation sets its own standards, and one company will look for candidates another tries to avoid. Is it any wonder we find a "duke's mixture" of talents and personalities in the ranks of middle management?

Take that down to a department level in a corporation. One person flourishes in a given atmosphere, and another can't tolerate it. I may work well under your supervision but fail miserably under someone else's. I recall taking on a young man from another department to work in mine. My reference checks with the candidate's former management drew nothing but praise—hard worker, innovative, alert to the needs of the business, and so on. You know the line. Six months after the young man was placed on our staff, I ran into one of his former bosses. "So you took on Harold," he said. "What a stumblebum that guy is! Surprised you can put up with him."

Now, I thought my new man was pretty good. He was, in my opinion, everything the reference checks had said he was. We had given him some instruction when he first came on board, and he was placed under another supervisor who worked closely with him. All I heard was how capable and how diligent the man was. Here, now, was a former employer giving me quite a different picture. I told the former manager that I was pleased with what I had seen so far. "Well, good luck," he replied. "Some can pick 'em, and some can't."

"That's true," I said, "but if Harold succeeds, you'll know that some can manage, and some can't." It might have been a low blow, but I don't think the man heard it. He wasn't much of a listener, either.

We contend that to manage takes brains. I said that to a manager one day, and his reply was, "Anyone who had brains would never get into this business!" Intelligence is always looked for in selecting a manager, but we all know intelligent people who don't manage very well. Take Steinmetz, the little genius who made all of Tom Edison's inventions work. He was hired at General Electric to manage a research laboratory but was such an avid scientist that he paid no attention to managing. The company set up a little lab for him and let him do what he wanted. Without doubt, the person who managed *him* wasn't nearly as intelligent as Steinmetz, but he was a better manager. You've seen that happen in a lesser way in your company—the competent managing the brilliant.

Name other attributes often accorded managers—strength, courage, imagination, thoroughness, positive attitudes, good appearance. They all count, and the more you have of each, the better you are. Yet there are some people who have these attributes but can't manage, and there are others who lack a few but are really quite competent at the head of an organization. Even the best education in business doesn't assure success; we've all seen the MBA with accounting awards and case-study merit badges who couldn't make the wheels turn and the high school dropout who could.

A recent *Wall Street Journal* article (January 13, 1982) by Erik Larson reported some interesting findings by Charles A. Garfield, president of Peak Performance Center, Berkeley, California, and clinical professor at the medical school, University of California at

San Francisco. Garfield describes high performers as having unique skills, work habits, and methods of coping with stress and risks. They are, in his words, "different folks." Although most of what he says applies to the very top levels of managers, it can help us learn something about the potential that exists in the ranks of middle managers. After all, those who are at the top got there via the middle.

Here are six characteristics that, according to Garfield, are the marks of top performers:

○ They are able to go beyond previous levels of accomplishment.
○ They avoid the comfort zone—don't "feel at home" where they are.
○ They do things for the art of it—have internal goals.
○ They solve problems rather than place blame.
○ They confidently take risks after appraising the worst consequences.
○ They are able to rehearse coming actions mentally.

I mention this body of research for two reasons: It supports previous statements made in this book—findings of other earlier behavioral scientists—and it also suggests that those of us in middle management would do well to keep a weather eye open for ourselves and our subordinates. It could be that we're overlooking capabilities—our own or someone else's—that, properly harnessed, could be the start of something big!

Lay these characteristics against the list of middle management complaints, and you'll see interesting parallels. Middle managers want to have the opportunity to show that they can do more than they're presently being allowed to. "I wouldn't let Ted try to handle that; he'd fall flat on his face." Often the manager steers opportunities *away* from certain subordinates, because failure is predicted. By whom? By the manager, not the subordinate. How serious are the consequences of failure? Could an attempt that didn't come off perfectly be corrected at midstream? If the project did blow, is there no road back? Look down the list of Garfield's characteristics of outstanding performers, and you'll discover that the really top people can look ahead, see consequences, rehearse the action, and take risks. Doesn't that tell us that really good managers should take a chance on a subordinate's trying and failing just to see what will happen?

And what are the consequences of failure to the subordinate? They can be many or few, great or insignificant. *How the manager treats the failure is the key issue.* If the manager does whatever he or she can to forestall failure by working with the subordinate to make the project come off, chances are failure will be marginal or will never occur. And if it does occur? I've tried to accept failures of those about me with the grace with which I expect them to accept my failures. We all fail at something. That's not what we fear; we fear the criticism that rises out of failure. That, unfortunately, is what keeps us from trying to do even the things we might succeed at. And so the vicious circle of low productivity is formed.

To form the upward spiral of high productivity, managers have to take risks on what subordinates are capable of doing by giving them the opportunity to *try*—and to fail, if need be. I have always viewed with some suspicion the old cliché, "You learn more from failure than from success." I'd rather learn from success, and experts will tell you that repeating success is a marvelous reinforcement of behavior. You can learn from failure, but only if you understand where the errors were, and what is the right course to take the next time around. Instruction rather than criticism is what we owe subordinates, and it is better-timed if it comes *before* and *during* the action than after it.

Another of Garfield's observations is that high performers avoid the comfort zone. You have middle managers under your supervision who seem quite content to be where they are. That doesn't trouble me if they remain productive and proud of ongoing achievements made at that level. It does trouble me if they rest on their oars and believe that past successes are all that count. How do you tell the difference? The plant manager who feels the shop is just great the way it is, who resists or doesn't look for opportunities to improve it, make it more productive, safer, more profitable, and more trouble-free is the coaster. The sales manager who sees new products as just another problem and who drags his or her feet when new techniques and routines are established is the camper. Staying on the same job isn't the problem, but *keeping the job the same is!* As managers, we have to recognize the difference—in ourselves and in others.

One way to know the difference is to measure the number of constructive suggestions offered by subordinates. "If we could just do this. . . ." "When are we going to be able to . . . ?" You can discover it in conversations. You can see it in forward plans and budget submissions. You can find it in intrastaff cooperation. Participative management is diagnostic as well as therapeutic.

The observation that the best performers have internal goals and like to achieve is the classic theme of the behavioral scientists. That truth is played out daily in today's business world, with managers who leave one company and go to another in order to satisfy those internal needs. My own conclusion is that such movement is not so much a quest for fulfillment of goals as an attempt to find a manager who will make that fulfillment possible. Too often we think of ourselves as achievers without also recognizing that those for whom we have a managerial responsibility are likewise achievers waiting for the opportunity.

We live in a remarkable age. Change seems to be both inevitable and desirable. What distinguishes this age from earlier ones is that for centuries the style of management stood still, although the technology that was managed changed dramatically. The pioneers of industry were the inventors and the people who could bring those inventions to the marketplace. They were movers and shakers and a step ahead of those they led. In most cases, their successes came early, and they enjoyed prominence and wealth that set them apart from the crowd. Their concept of paying off social indebtedness was that their own success created jobs below, and that settled the account. It's unlikely that they ever considered the many things we discuss in our time about management style and technique.

Educational opportunities, once reserved for the very rich, became available to more and more people. Less than a century ago, the high school diploma was the sine qua non of educational achievement. A half century ago, it still meant a little, but not as much as it had. The post-World War II period put the "peasants" in the classroom right next to the offspring of the entrepreneurs and the managerial class. The growth of technology paralleled the growth in the numbers of educated and expectant candidates for leadership roles. There were people walking away from the commencement platform with diplomas they perceived as first-class tickets to corporate boardrooms. And these were men and women whose parents retained ingrained respect for anyone who worked in an office, wore a suit, carried a briefcase, or walked past a time clock without punching it. What a turnaround!

As the new managerial candidates were absorbed into the business scene, however, they discovered that the more there were of them, the less revered they seemed to be. The meteoric rise some of them had expected just wasn't there. They began to discover that people didn't listen to managers just because they were managers; managers who were listened to were those who had something to say. They also discovered that when they couldn't control by exerting power, they could get things done by gaining cooperation. Although managerial power still plays a strong role in many ways, it has given way to style and technique. The old days are gone forever.

We find ourselves in other circumstances in this decade of change. Mergers and acquisitions and consolidations are changing what were once comfortable and seemingly unassailable managerial relationships. The manufacturing facility that was once so vital is now obsolete, and the corporation chooses to close it rather than refurbish it. Women are moving from the clerical force to supervisory and management roles and invading the executive suite and boardroom. Automation is replacing not only the plant worker but the office worker as well. How can we help but move in new directions with our management attitudes and actions?

Not every manager, not every company will move in the same direction or at the same speed. Here are two expressions from key executives in the same industry, facing the same problem at the same time. One calls himself an aggressive peacemaker and points to the need for programs of internal communication to help solve problems in the workplace. "Today's work force is better educated and expectations are greater," he says. "The capacity for dissent is there . . . management must do a lot more selling of ideas than mandating performance." He is a successful executive representing a company that has known great success.

His counterpart across town is described by those who know him and have worked with him as one who has for years "been seeking the advice of the guy on the line." The executive says of himself that he "learned to listen to the person closest to the job when the time came to solve problems." He is his company's foremost advocate of quality of worklife and the policy of sharing decision-making responsibilities with lower-ranking employees. He, too, is a successful executive representing a company that has known great success.

Both executives are going in the right direction, but the second is far ahead of the first. The first talks about *selling* management ideas. That, indeed, is necessary. But the second talks about *discovering* ideas. I'll wager that the *discovered* idea is easier to sell than the one created in the manager's office. And when it comes to listening to the person closest to the problem and sharing in the making of decisions, middle managers in the second company have a lot more fun than those in the first.

One of the marks of maturity is one's ability to move with change, to adapt to it, to harness it, and to become an agent of even further change. The newer styles of management are more open, more participative, and more receptive to ideas from below. Crises have forced many companies to jump into the style—presidents of companies and presidents of unions getting their heads together in last-minute bail-out campaigns. What a waste, when all along there has existed the instrument for preventing crisis—a properly employed, fully informed, entirely competent, and self-directing middle management.

Managers at all levels must recognize that the intriguing thing about human resources, as opposed to all other resources, is that the more they are properly used, the more they grow in value. What a human resource may not be able to do, it can be taught to do. What it cannot do by itself, it may be able to do with complementary resources. The most limiting factor in the realm of human resources is the manager who has been given control over them.

As we seek productivity in others, we will do better to develop competence than to apply controls. The more deserved recognition we accord, the more recognizable the performance will be. The more self-sufficiency we encourage, the more we'll get. The more cooperation we foster, the greater it will be. If we are to *get* people to achieve, we have to *let* them, *help* them, and *support* them. The people who report to you want precisely what you want for yourself, and it is so simple to give them that.

Your company doesn't have to subscribe to a corporationwide style dictated by policy or subscribed to with religious fervor. It can start in your own department, with the five or six managers or supervisors who call you their boss. You can be sure that once you get it going, it won't stop there.

The Chinese philosopher Lao-tse, who lived back in about 550 B.C., offered a perceptive observation about modern management, even though he never had to cope with it:

A leader is best when people barely know he exists. Not so good when people obey and acclaim him. Worse when they despise him. But of a good leader who talks little, when his work is done, his aim fulfilled, they will say, "We did it ourselves."

That's what middle managers want to be able to say. *Let them!*

Index

ability
    importance of, in delegation,
        65
    see also competence
accelerated promotion, as af-
    fecting women managers,
        121–122
account, expense, 81–82
accountability
    as problem area in middle
        management, 14
    see also responsibility(ies)
achievement(s)
    as defined by job descriptions,
        89–90
    goals as measures of, 32, 212
    as means of motivation, 83
    -motivated managers, 24
    needs, as defined by Maslow's
        hierarchy of needs, 9
    -oriented managers, 40
    as satisfier, 172
    training as affecting, 129
acquisitions, as creating change,
        228–229
activity reports, as time-saving
    tool, 105
advancement
    barriers to, 56
    encouragement of, 54
    restrictions in, 15

see also opportunity; promo-
    tions
advice, seeking, 41–50
    in suggestion-gathering process,
        219
    see also counseling
agencies, as aiding in skill devel-
    opment, 128
agenda, use of, in staff meetings,
        194
ambition, recognition of, through
    career counseling, 58–59
American Management Associa-
    tions, business courses of,
        128
analysis, training needs, 126
announcements
    communication of, 191
    see also information
apologies, avoidance of, through
    in-house consultations, 49
approval
    competition for, among subor-
        dinates, 71
    support and, 115–116
art, management as, 223–230
Art of Japanese Management, The
    (Pascale), 145
assignment of tasks
    historical overview of, 29
    as managerial function, 31

assistants
  historical development of, 29
  see also subordinates
associates, as aids in career planning, 57–58
Athos, Anthony, on Japanese management, 145
attention, as element in listening process, 48
attitudes, as factor determining performance, 119
attrition, 25
audiences
  classification of, 132
  as performance judges, 190
authoritative management styles, 148, 149–150
authority
  as element in job description, 92
  formal *vs.* real, 172
  lack of, as problem in delegation, 63–64
  responsibility and, 14
  sharing of, in participative management, 162–163
  support and, 115–116
  automation, as creating change, 229

behavior, inheritance of, in managerial hierarchy, 8–9
behavioral science
  historical overview of, 167–175
  managerial personalities as viewed by, 33–34
  motivation as studied by, 83
  top performers as analyzed by, 224–225
benefits (compensatory)
  age discrimination and, 79
  as dissatisfiers, 75

inequities in, as concern to middle management, 15
performance as related to, 84–96
see also compensation programs
benefits (rewards)
  of career counseling, 59
  of creating job descriptions, 95–96
  of communication, 138
  of delegation, 70–71
  as reward system, 72–73
  of training, 129–130
  see also rewards
benevolent authoritative management style, 148, 149–150
Blumenthal, Michael W., 43
bonus plans, as reward system, 74
brainstorming, use of, in participative sessions, 181
bunching of calls, as time management technique, 106
business, small
  management of, 6
  style of management, 148–149
business life *vs.* personal life, 105

capability
  as factor determining performance, 119
  see also ability
career planning, 52–54
  application of program for, 55–60
  mid-, problems related to, 79
cause, identification of, for problem-solving routine, 203–204
challenge, as standard for goal setting, 212
change, as affecting management, 227–230

chart, organization
    historical overview of, 29
    problems associated with,
        89–90
clarity, importance of, in partici-
    pative management, 222
closed questions, 182
coaching, see counseling; training
colleges
    as affecting development of
        management structure, 6–7,
        224
    as aiding in skill development,
        128
    lack of, as promotion barrier,
        56
    see also education
comfort zone, avoidance of, by
    top performers, 225–227
commitment, participative ses-
    sions as concluding with,
    184
common sense, as approach to
    problem solving, 201
communication
    control of, 134–135
    delegation as relying on, 64–65
    effective, guidelines for,
        135–138
    equitable treatment of employ-
        ees as relying on, 77, 80–83
    flawed, in improper delegation,
        99
    historical overview of, 132–135
    through meetings, see meetings
    open, 133–134
    process, improving, 36
    questioning problems as related
        to, 46–47
    of salary plans, 73–74
    skills, as enrichment area for
        middle managers, 128

technology as affecting, 120,
    133
theories, 13
training process as requiring,
    129–130
of work assignments, 87
compensation programs
    communication of, 77, 80–83
    equity problems related to,
        78–80
    see also benefits (compensatory)
competence
    gaining, through delegation, 66
    see also ability
complaints, participative manage-
    ment as answering, 160
compliments, delivery of, in per-
    formance appraisals, 94
computer age, effect of, on deci-
    sion making, 202
conditions, identification of, for
    problem-solving routine,
    202–203
conditions-have-changed ap-
    proach, in suggestion-gath-
    ering process, 219–220
confidence
    need for, in presenting ideas,
        218
    providing, through support,
        117
    see also worth, personal
confidentiality, establishing in
    communication process, 136
conflicts, inner-office, as caused
    by office arrangements,
        76–77
consolidations, as creating
    change, 228–229
constructive questioning, 47
consultative management style,
    148, 150

consultative management style
(*cont.*)
see also participative management
consulting
as aid in skill development, 128
of in-house personnel, 41–50
organizations, use of, 126
Japanese management as, 145
see also counseling
continuing training, 123
see also education
contributing, importance of, in
problem-solving, 206–207
control
achieving, through communication, 139
American management as rely-
ing on, 145
maintaining, during staff meetings, 199
as managerial responsibility, 61
cooperation, Japanese reliance
on, 145
counseling
application of program for,
55–60
career, 58
in goal setting, 211–212
management, 53–54
progression problems as aided
by, 52–54
as skill requirement of participative management, 179–189
see also consulting
country boy, as personality classification, 196
courage, lack of, as hindering
support, 117
courier service, as improvement
in communication process,
133

courtesy, as related to productivity, 107
creativity
elements inhibiting, 181
encouragement of, through delegation, 70
lack of support as hindering,
110
questioning as provoking, 182
criticism
avoidance of, through in-house
consultation, 50
see also recommendations

Dallas, 11
data processing
as affecting decision making,
202
historical development of, 30
technology as affecting, 120
decision making
as enrichment skill for middle
managers, 128
as managerial skill, 34
as problem area in middle
management, 15
skill development of, through
delegation, 71
systems of, 200–201
step-by-step routine for,
202–207
see also problem solving
delegation
elements of, 50, 63–64
managerial success as affected
by, 62
steps in, 69–70
subordinate involvement in, 65
see also participative management
description, job, *see* job description

Detroit Free Press, 43, 145
direct approach, in suggestion-
    gathering process, 218–219
direction
    establishing, through objec-
        tives, 180–181
    lack of, as problem in middle
        management, 14
    providing, as managerial skill,
        34, 65
directive management
    in American management, 145
    as hiding management quali-
        ties, 163
    problems of, 99, 146–147
discipline
    as managerial responsibility, 61
    in participative management,
        181–182
    use of, in time management,
        105–106
    see also punishments
disclaimer, in job descriptions, 85
discrimination, age, 79
discussion leadership, 164
dissatisfiers, as defined by Freder-
    ick Herzberg, 75, 171–172
Donnelly, John, 153–154
double standards, in management
    hierarchy, 13–14
Douglass, Merrill, on time man-
    agement, 99–100
drafts, use of, for goal setting,
    209–210
Drucker, Peter, on management,
    144
Dynasty, 12

economists, views of decision
    making by, 205
Edison, Thomas, 158
education

accessibility of, 228
    as affecting management, 224
    of managers, 23–24
    see also colleges
ego
    needs, 9
    satisfaction, 169
emergencies, handling of, through
    training, 127
Empirical Law of Effect, 168
employees
    classifications of, 195–197
    loss of, 3
    pass through, 21
    recruiting of, by General Elec-
        tric Company, 53
enrichment skills, managerial, 128
equitability, 72–83
errands, as interrupting workflow,
    97–98
esteem
    need for, 169
    see also confidence
evaluation, job
    disclaimer lines as affecting, 85
    see also performance, apprais-
        als
Executive Suite, 11
expectation
    clashes of, as problem of inter-
        management, 17
    see also goals
expense accounts, communica-
    tion, of, 81–82
experience, work, as affecting
    promotion, 56
expert(s)
    as personality classification,
        196
    see also specialists
exploitative authoritative man-
    agement style, 148, 149–150

failure, treatment of, by managers, 226
feedback
  as replacing performance review, 91
  see also communication
final drafts, use of, in forward planning, 210
first drafts, use of, in forward planning, 210
followers, as defined by Rensis Likert, 5, 8
formal authority, 172
format
  of communications, 136
  for goal-setting planning, 209
  job description, 92
forward planning, use of, in goal setting, 208–214
Fraser, Doug, 156
freedom, encouragement of, through delegation, 70
full delegation, as phase of delegation process, 64, 66
function, as element in job description, 92

Garfield, Charles A., on performance, 224–225
goal(s)
  clashes of, as problem of inter-management, 17
  internal, of top performers, 225, 227
  management's responsibility related to, 32–33
  -oriented managers, 24
  setting, through participative management, 34–40, 65, 183, 208–214
  skill-development as related to, 128

standards for, 211–212
  see also objectives
grade/salary-range system, 72–73
  as consideration in compensation system, 78–80
  relationship of, to performance and job description, 84–96
groups
  meetings for, 193–194
  study of, 167–168
growth
  restrictions in, 15
  as satisfier, 172
  see also advancement

habit, as causing management problems, 65
Hawthorne experiment, 151
  as genesis of behavioral science, 167–168
Herzberg, Frederick, on compensation systems, 75–76, 171–172
hierarchy of needs (Maslow), 9, 168–169
hitchhiker, as personality classification, 197
home-study education programs, 128
house organs, as traditional communications tool, 131–132
Human Side of Enterprise (McGregor), 170

Iacocca, Lee, 43–44
incompetence
  delegation problems as causing, 62–63
  Peter Principle and, 121
increases
  as consideration in compensation program, 78–80

merit, as resolving pay inequities, 75
indirect approach, in suggestion-gathering process, 219
Industrial Revolution, 29
industry
    automotive, 23
    change within, 227–230
    historical overview of, 29–30
information
    classifications of, 132
    generating of, see meetings
    lack of, as problem in middle management, 14
    privileged, 135
    seeking, through questioning, 46–47
    see also announcements
inner office conflicts, as caused by office arrangements, 76–77
input, 46
    see also suggestions
insight, gaining, through questioning, 48–49
instruction, see training
interaction-influence principle, 172
interest
    displayment of, in subordinates, 56
    mutual, as key in Japanese management, 145
intermanagement, problems related to, 17–20
interruptions
    avoidance of, as element in listening process, 48
    as hindering creativity, 181
    as managerial complaint, 97–108
intuition, as approach to problem solving, 201

involvement
    in management function, 41–50
    see also participative management

Japanese industry, management approach of, 144–145
job(s)
    difficulty of, 119–121
    personnel filling, 121–122
    talent problems related to, 122–127
job description
    developing, steps for, 91–93
    historical overview of, 29
    relationship of, to performance and job grade, 84–91
    rewriting, 73
job rotation
    as employed by General Electric Company, 53
    see also movement
judgment
    importance of, in delegation, 65
    as managerial skill, 31
    and power, 99
    withholding, 183

language, use of, in job descriptions, 92
Lao-tse, on leadership, 230
Larson, Erik, on performance, 224–225
last-line disclaimer, in job descriptions, 85
Law of Effect, Empirical, 168
leaders, as defined by Rensis Likert, 5, 8
Likert, Rensis, 4–5, 8, 35, 75, 148, 172–173

limitations
  on discussion, 181
  managerial, 34
limited delegation, as phase of
    delegation process, 63–64, 66
line workers
  management problems as re-
      lated to, 5
  roles of, 9
  scientific management and, 30
linking-pin concept, 4–5, 8, 35,
    172
listening
  importance of, in participative
      management, 45–46, 222
  process, 48–49
logs, maintenance of, for perform-
    ance appraisals, 94
long-range solutions to business
    problems, 205
loyalty
  achieving, through communica-
      tion, 139
  assurance of, 54
  training ability as related to,
      127
  see also trust

McGregor, Douglas
  on managerial power, 75, 145
  on Theory X and Theory Y, 170
machine-dependent operations,
    119
management
  American vs. Japanese,
      144–145
  art of, 223–230
  directive, 99
  equity as concern of, 74–75
  hierarchy, 8–9
  historical overview of, 29–33,
      61

linking-pin concept of, 5, 8, 35
managers and, see manager(s)
participative, see participative
    management
poor, results of, 3–4, 11
reform, 91
science of, 223–230
style, 143–144, 148
time, 99–100, 108
Management by Participation,
    151
manager(s)
  consulting of in-house staff by,
      41–50
  -controlled process, 159
  -dominated process, 159
  education level of, 23–24, 31
  as evaluators of training needs,
      123
  job descriptions as responsibil-
      ity of, 85–96
  judgment of, 31
  middle, see managers, middle
  office arrangements as concern
      of, 76–77
  owners as, 29
  personality traits of, 33–34
  qualities of, 223–230
  salary concerns of, 72–75
  task assignment as role of, 31
  top, see managers, top
  training provided by, 119–
      130
  women, problems related to,
      121–122
managers, middle
  communication problems of,
      132–149
  complaints of, 14–15, 33, 61
  defined, 4–9, 16
  enrichment areas for, 127–
      130

goals of, 32–33
importance of, 20–21, 36–37
management problems related
to, 4, 12–13
management style as affecting,
143–157
participative management and,
see participative management
salary concerns of, 72–73
support from, 109–113
see also manager(s)
managers, top
problems related to, 4, 12–13,
15
providing support as role of,
116–118
role of, 9
task-oriented, 33
see also manager(s)
Managerial Grid (Blake-Mouton),
173
*Manage Your Time, Manage Your
Work, Manage Your Life*
(Douglass), 99–100
manipulative psychology, 167
manuals, policy, 84
Maslow, Abraham, 9, 168–169
May, Elton, 151, 167
measurability of goals, 212
media, effect of, on communication, 131
meetings
as communications tool,
131–132
conducting, 190–199
as process in participative management, 159, 179–189
superfluous, as interrupting
workflow, 97–98
training, 123–124
see also reviews

mergers, as creating change,
228–229
merit increases
as consideration in compensation system, 78–80
as resolving pay inequities,
75
messenger service, as improvement in communication process, 133
midcareer problems, 79
middle managers, *see* managers,
middle
misunderstanding
management problems caused
by, 63
in questioning, 46
money
as reward for accomplishment,
33
see also salary
monitoring, job description,
86–87
see also review, job description
monthly reports, as time-saving
tool, 105
motivation
as enrichment skill for middle
managers, 128
in goal setting, 211
levels of, 9
money as source of, 75
problems related to, 13–14
theory, 164, 166–175
as threat to managerial position, 51–52
training as aiding in, 127
motives
achievement, 24
clashes of, 17
creating, through counseling,
59

movement
  inter-company, 25
  see also job rotation

National Society of Sales Training
    Executives, 195
needs
  developmental, 163
  hierarchy of, 9, 168–169
  training, 126
negotiating, as managerial skill,
    34
Network, 11
Nine to Five, 11
notes
  appraisal, 94, 194
  technique of taking, 49

objectives
  defining, in staff meetings,
    193–194
  delegation as related to, 65
  historical overview of, 29
  management by, 44
  participative management and,
    see participative manage-
    ment
Odiorne, George, 44
office arrangements, inequities in,
    76–77
one-to-one exchange
  importance of, 192
  as process in participative man-
    agement, 192
open communication, 133–134
open-door policy, use of, in time
    management, 106
open management, *see* participa-
    tive management
open questions, use of, in counsel-
    ing sessions, 182

opportunity
  displaying, in career counsel-
    ing, 55
  -oriented personnel, 51
  restrictions in, 15
  see also advancement; promo-
    tion
oral explanation, as communica-
    tions format, 136
orders, management, 85
organization chart, 13
  historical overview of, 29
  problems associated with,
    89–90
organizational development, *see*
    participative management
organizing, as managerial skill, 34
Ouchi, William, on Japanese
    management, 145
oversupervision
  direction as causing, 65
  as management complaint, 14,
    33, 61
  problems of, 22
owners, 29

Paradise Lost, 107
parent/child relationship, 93
participation in training sessions,
    124
participative management
  benefits of, 158–165
  consulting of in-house person-
    nel as element in, 34–50,
    148, 150–157
  defined, 159
  delegation, as element of, 65
  effectiveness of, 147–157
  installing, 158, 163–165
  Japanese as utilizing, 144–147
  skill requirements for promot-
    ing, 179–189

suggestions, as integral part of, 215–222
Pascale, Richard, on Japanese management, 145–146
pass-through personnel, 21
paternalistic organization, management style of, 148
patience, importance of, in suggestion-gathering process, 221
peer approval, competition for, by subordinates, 71
pensions, age discrimination and, 79
perfection, as aim of management decision, 206
performance
    appraisals, 85, 91–96
    characteristics of top, 225
    factors affecting, 119
    recognition of, 24–25, 61
    relationship of, to job grade and description, 84–89
    -review sessions, 57, 91
permanence, as aim of management decision, 206
personality classifications, 196–197
personal life vs. business life, 105
personnel department, 85–87
Peter Principle, 121
philosophers, general discussion on, 167
physical needs, 9
physical office arrangements, inequities in, 76–77
physiological needs, 169
planning
    forward, 208–214
    historical overview of, 29–30
    as managerial skill, 34

participative management as utilizing, 159
strategic vs. tactical, 35
point, grade, as consideration in compensation system, 78–80
policy
    administering of, 77
    as dissatisfier, 172
    manuals, 84
politician, as personality classification, 196
position
    as reward for accomplishment, 33
    see also job(s)
power
    Douglas McGregor on, 75
    effect of in-house consultation on, 41, 46
    in managerial hierarchy, 8–9
    misdirected, 99–108
    problems of, 33
praise, as compensation for salary reward, 75
preparation, importance of, in participative management, 222
prestige, as reward for accomplishment, 33
privilege, managerial, abuse of, 98
privileged information, 135
probe, as element in listening process, 48–49
problem evaluation, as step in problem-solving routine, 204
problem solving
    as enrichment skill, 128
    participative counseling sessions as tool for, 183
    step-by-step routine for, 202–207

problem solving (*cont.*)
  systems of, 200–201
  see also decision making
productivity
  management as affecting, 13,
    143–145
  in participative management
    meetings, 181
Professional Manager, The
  (McGregor), 75
progression system, career planning as, 53
promises, avoidance of, in career
  planning, 56–57
promotions
  accelerated, as affecting
    women managers, 121–122
  barriers to, 56
  performance as related to, 84
  see also advancement
proposals, *see* recommendations
protocol, as related to productivity, 107
provisional delegation, as phase
  of delegation process, 64,
  66
psychology
  as affecting development of
    management structure, 6–7
  managerial, as enrichment skill,
    128
  manipulative, 167
publications, employee, as traditional communications tool,
  131–132
punishments
  as affecting behavior, 168
  as related to power, 75
  as standard for goal setting, 212
  see also discipline
purpose, statement of, importance of, 46–47

quality, product, 31
quantity, product, 31
questions
  asking of, 45–46
  importance of, in counseling
    sessions, 182–183
  problems related to, 146–
    147
  samples of, 47
  use of, in problem-solving rou-
    tine, 204
quizzing, avoidance of, in questioning, 48
quotas
  handling of, 208
  see also goal(s)

Rapp, Jim, on participation in
  meetings, 195
real authority, 172
rebuttals, avoidance of, during listening process, 49
recognition
  enrichment skills as affecting,
    127–129
  lack of, 51
  of performance, 24–25
  as reward for accomplishment,
    33
  as satisfier, 172
  signs of, in meetings, 49
recommendations
  application of, in participative
    management, 183
  instruction in formulating,
    215–222
  see also criticism
recruiting, by General Electric
  Company, 53
regrading, job, *see* job description; grade/salary-range system

relationships
  as element in job descriptions,
    92
  improving, through participa-
    tive management, 165
  management, 24–25
  parent/child, 93
report(s), activity, as time-saving
  tool, 105
reporting, participative management as utilizing, 159
resentment, 34
resignations, 3
respect
  achieving, through communica-
    tions, 138
  importance of, 107–108
response(s)
  recognition signs in, 49
  -seeking questions, 47, 182–
    183
  see also recommendations
responsibility(ies)
  acceptance of, 24
  authority and, 14
  communication as related to,
    132
  creating, through support, 117
  as element in job descriptions,
    92
  gaining, through delegation, 66
  ill-defined, as resulting from job
    description disclaimer, 92
  as satisfier, 172
  sharing of, in participative
    management, 162–163
restrictions
  managerial, 34
  see also limitations
result-seeking questions, 47
review sessions
  job description, 85–86

performance, 57
  see also meetings
reward(s)
  as affecting behavior, 168
  importance of, 72
  as managerial responsibility, 61
  pay plans as means of, 72–76
  as standard for goal setting, 212
  see also benefits (rewards)
risk taking, 110
role play, illustrative participative session commitment,
  184–189
rooms, selection of, for staff meetings, 195
rotation, job, as employed by
  General Electric Company,
  53
rumors, guidelines for handling,
  137–138

safety, 31
  needs, 169
  see also security
salary(ies)
  communication of, 80–83
  as dissatisfiers, 172
  inequities in, as concern to
    middle management, 15
  plans, as reward system, 72–76
  see also money
Sales & Marketing Management
  Magazine, 195
salesmanship, importance of, in
  suggestion-gathering process,
  221
sandbagger, as personality classification, 196–197
satisfaction, ego, 169
satisfiers, as defined by Frederick
  Herzberg, 171–172
Scanlon, Joseph, 153–154

Scanlon Plan, 153
schedules, maintaining, through
    time management, 105
science, management as, 223–
    230
second drafts, use of, in forward
    planning, 210
secretaries, 80
security, 9
    as dissatisfier, 172
    see also safety
self-actualization, 169
shop-operations, job simplicity
    programs as affecting, 119
short-range solutions to business
    problems, 205
simplicity
    job, failure of programs for,
        119–120
    use of, in job descriptions, 92
skill(s)
    -dependent operations, 119
    development of, 71
    enrichment, 127–128
    requirements for participative
        management, 179–189
    updating, 128–130
small business, management of,
    5
Smith, Adam, 30
Smith, Homer, on meetings, 195
social needs, 9, 169
solutions
    recognition of, 204–205
    see also problem solving
speaking, as managerial skill, 34
specialists
    consulting of, 41–50
    historical development of, 30
specific training, 123
standards, in management hierar-
    chy, 13–14

status, as dissatisfier, 172
strategic planning, *vs.* tactical
    planning, 35
strength
    consulting as, 41
    see also power
study programs, home, 128
style
    as element in recommenda-
        tions, 216, 218–221
    management, 41–42
subjects, meeting, selection of,
    194
subordinates
    career counseling of, 52–54,
        55–60
    as consultants, 41–50
    delegation as involving, 65
    involvement of, in managerial
        responsibilities, 34–40
    participative management as
        accepted by, 161–162
substance, as element in recom-
    mendations, 216–218
success
    personal and company, 34,
        49
    see also achievements
suggestions
    application of, in participative
        management, 183
    instruction in formulating,
        215–222
    see also recommendations
summarizing statement, use of, in
    listening process, 49
supervision
    as dissatisfier, 172
    problems of, 14
support
    importance of, 109–113
    lack of, 15

as managerial responsibility, 65
supportive-relationship principle, 172–173
survey, training needs, 126
see also reviews

tactical planning, *vs.* strategic planning, 35
talent
  displaying, through participative management, 159
  job placement problems and, 122
targets, in goal setting, 210–211
tasks
  assignment of, 29
  goals as affecting, 31–32
  job descriptions as listing, 90
  as managerial function, 31, 61
  -oriented managers, 33
  vs. role, 171
Taylor, Frederick W., on scientific management, 30
teacher/learner relationship, 93
team building, *see* participative management
technological revolution
  as affecting development of management structure, 6, 120–121
  skill updating and, 128–130
telecommunications, as improvement in communications process, 133
telephone calls, bunching of, 106
testing, avoidance of, in questioning, 47
Theory X and Theory Y (McGregor), 163, 170, 179
Theory Z, as Japanese approach to management, 145

Theory Z: How American Business Can Meet the Japanese Challenge (Ouchi), 145
Thorndike, E. L., on learning, 168
threats
  to authority, 51–56
  as causing delegation problems, 62–63
  ideas as, 217–218
time
  allocation of, for performance appraisals, 94
  as element in compensation system, 78–80
  management, 99–108
  saving of, 50
  wasters, 97–99, 181
timetable, use of, in staff meetings, 194
title, as element in job description, 92
top-down management style, 148
top managers, *see* mangers, top
training
  as aiding delegation, 65–66
  areas of concern in, 123–130
  changes in, need for, 121
  discipline and, 183
  needs analysis, 45, 126
  organizations, 123–124
  problems of, 14
  traps, questions as, 46–47
trust
  cultivating, among subordinates, 137
  manager's desire for, 135
  see also loyalty
Tulip Time town, 152–153
turnover
  controlling, 3

turnover (*cont.*)
  in managerial positions, 11–12,
    24

underdevelopment of managers,
    24
understanding, lack of, 17–22
undersupervision
  direction as aiding, 65
  problems of, 14, 21–22, 61
unions
  as affecting communication,
    131
  contracts, rewards and, 72
  equitable payment as concern
    of, 75
United Auto Workers, 23
university(ies)
  as aiding skill development,
    128
  see also education
University of Michigan's Institute
    for Social Research, 148, 150,
    173
updating, skill, 128–129
upgrading, *see* job description
urgent, as task classification,
    99–104

values, shared, as key in Japanese
    management, 145

Wall Street Journal, 224
Wealth of Nations (Smith), 30
weekly reports, as time-saving
    tool, 105

wet puppy, as personality classifi-
    cation, 197
women managers
  accelerated promotion as af-
    fecting; 121–122
  changing role of, 228–229
word notes, 49
work assignments, communica-
    tion of, 87
work experience, lack of, as pro-
    motion barrier, 56
workflow, 97–98
work groups, study of, as related
    to productivity, 167
workload, delegation as balanc-
    ing, 70
work planning, participative
    counseling sessions as tool
    for, 183
World War II era, changes dur-
    ing, 7
worth, personal, 49
  delegation as increasing, 70
  as jeopardized by supervisory
    problems, 62
  job description as increasing,
    95
  training as affecting, 129
  see also confidence
written explanation
  as communication format,
    136
  use of, in communication pro-
    cess, 159

zones, comfort, 225–227